"I Just Want My Life Back"

From Trauma To Triumph

Carrie L. Reichartz

ISBN: 978-0-9859456-2-6

CIP DATA: sexual abuse, rape, memoir

Individuals and groups may order books from Carrie Reichartz directly, or from the publisher. Retailers and wholesalers should order from our distributors.

Published by:
Infinitely More Life Publishing
P.O. Box 510376
New Berlin, WI 53151
414-916-5435
Website: InfinitelyMoreLife.org
    MercysLight.org

Email: carrie@infinitelymorelife.org

TABLE OF CONTENTS

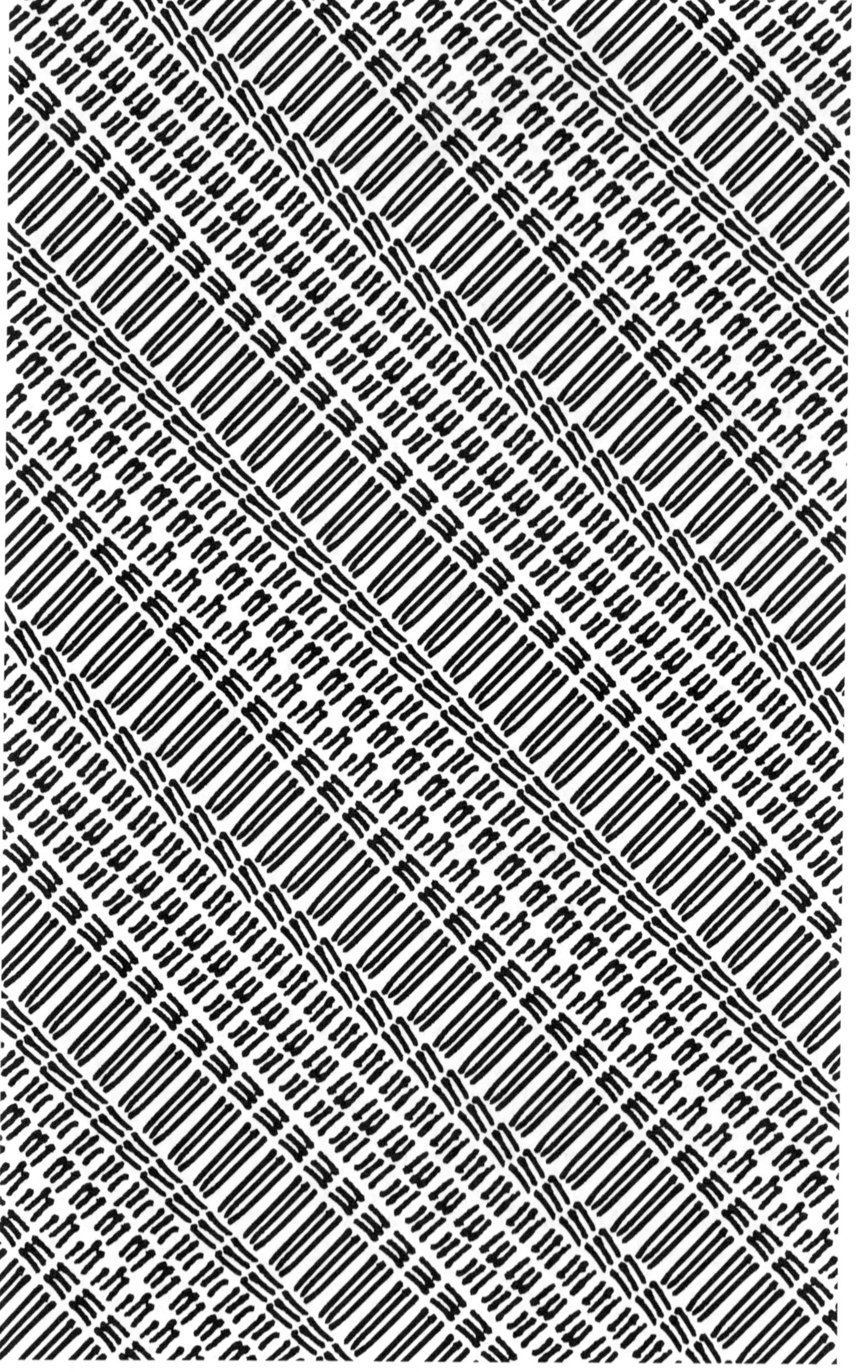

DEDICATED TO:

Elisha, for sharing her experience, which showed me the need for this book in 2012 and got me started.

Misty, a homeless girl, who showed me how others suffer through trauma to get me focused to finish in 2017.

Redeem and Restore Center video on human trafficking, which again showed me how lucky I have been through my trauma and how others are not.

For the principal at a local school, who would not allow a flyer to be distributed with the bad words of "rape" or "incest" on it – reminding me of how much the silence still exists.

Silence, protecting the perpetrators, while 1 in 4 of the girls sitting in his school are affected by incest and raped in his school but silence….

Silence – while we suffer alone….Silence

Those who will be silent no more….

Those who will take up the fight to see that another generation doesn't have to live through the same silence…

Thank you for your tremendous examples.

FORWARD

For over thirty years I have been helping sexual abuse survivors find healing and recover their joy. As a SA survivor myself, I knew the hyper-vigilance, the constant fear that something was wrong or would go wrong, and, at one point, the promiscuity that often is a part of a survivor's life. Every retreat I led helped me to heal. Sharing my story helped me to release the shame. I became proud of being resilient and eventually thriving and finding my joy again.

It was truly an honor to be a part of Carrie's journey. Witnessing her story and the release of old thwarted responses and emotion was powerful for all who were there. It was also a blessing to have Carrie on the support team at retreats and to watch her growth as she found her voice and her healing.

Now, I have tears in my eyes when I read her newsletters and watch her give so much to the world. She has truly taken healing to the next level through giving! I am proud to have been a part of her life and now to watch the love grow across the world.

Carrie's courage to tell her story is a gift, one that is given with great love and at the great cost of vulnerability. I pray that it will inspire you to reach out, to tell your story and get the love and support that is waiting for you to help you walk the path of healing. Let Carrie be your inspiration. Reach out. Carrie's message is that there are many who will walk with you, in your heart and at your side.

-Patricia Clason,
Emotional Intelligence Speaker, Corporate Coach,
Founder of Healing Warrior Health.

Author: *Claim Your Unlimited Potential* and *Speaking of Success* with Stephen Covey, Jack Canfield, Ken Blanchard and other books.

ACKNOWLEDGEMENTS

Thanks to all of you who made this possible.

My husband who is amazingly supportive of all I do.

My Mom and my dad.

Margaret Kline-Pofahl, Trillium Care Group, Elm Grove, Wisconsin for giving me guidance and direction through this, at times, agonizing journey.

Patricia Clason and the Center for Creative Learning, for changing my life from fear to love by showing me unconditional love.

Joyce Meyer, Beth Moore, and others, for sharing their experiences, which give me strength and courage to share mine.

Monica Heitman, for the first read and encouragement.

Timothy Lewis, for the second read and grammatical editing.

Chandra Hess, for graphic design of the cover, all her hours of volunteer help, and her final production of this book.

Jesi Espie, for her encouragement in this process.

Jesus, through Fox River Christian Church and many others, for accepting me for who I was and showing me a different way to do church and life.

Thank you, thank you, thank you!

PRELUDE...

When we defy, deny, or ignore our story, it defines us.
If we own it, we can rewrite the ending.
~Dr. Brene Brown

By addressing all areas of my life, fully evaluating each part, and acknowledging them, as the quote states above, I can rewrite the ending. This is even truer about trauma. If I don't address the trauma done to me, the people who hurt me will write it. I will remain stuck in my thoughts, fear, sadness, guilt, and shame, creating newer and bigger problems for me. I will cause trauma to others and even more to myself.

However, if I do address the trauma, I will be able to make decisions and take my life back. By doing this work, I can put the experiences where they belong–behind me. By doing this, I have found I can rewrite the ending. I hope this is what you are also looking to do. You can rewrite your ending. Your trauma doesn't need to be the end of your life. It doesn't need to define you.

I know some of you are thinking–this is impossible. Especially if you are on the beginning of your journey of healing, you feel like this will never be behind you. I know this feeling. Not too many years ago, I was there myself. But, I and many others are living proof that there is life after sexual abuse, rape, and trauma of any kind.

When you're starting or in the middle of your healing, it feels like your life is being consumed by trauma. It is all you think about and it feels like it is all you will ever think about. It feels like the only thing defining you.

It is true. Validate your feelings. Once you get through to the other side, life is much better, more fun, more exciting, and more free. This trauma does not define you. I promise you peace from your sorrow.

What do I hope to accomplish in reliving the past? My life was stolen from me at a very young age, then again in my preteens, in my teens, and continuing into my 30's, through my choices. This book, for me, is about taking my life back and also helping you take your life back. It's staring my areas of trauma right in the face and expressing them and sharing them with you. I poured my love into this book for you to fill your empty heart. I want you to know there is life after trauma. It can be a great life. I want you to know that you are loved, accepted, not forgotten, and are very important.

Come on my journey, through abuse, assault, rape, and trauma, to survivor, all the way to triumph. Along the way, you will find hope, inspiration, and courage to carry on with your journey from trauma to triumph.

Chapter 1

YOU ARE NOT ALONE

I write to give you hope, to let you know there is healing, a life, and even triumph, after trauma of any kind, even sexual trauma.

I write as a victim of trauma myself. When I was very young, I was sexually abused. In my preteen years, I was abused and raped. As a mid-teen, I was assaulted. When starting this journey, I didn't even realize how much the trauma had affected me. I thought I had done a good job of moving on, forgetting about the whole thing, and putting it behind me. I did not think it was affecting me in anyway. I ignored it and moved on. My life wasn't being affected by it. In fact, I didn't even think about it.

Looking back now, I realize that even after years of healing, it still affects me in areas of my life. Life isn't consumed by it anymore as it had been for many years, but it still has its effects. It was affecting me in ways I didn't even realize or acknowledge for over 20 years. I had been through:

- Bad and abusive relationships
- Terror with any positive male relationships in my life
- Almost dropping out of college
- An eight-year extremely broken marriage, filled with infidelity and addictions
- Divorce
- Huge mistakes that I wish, to this day, I could take back

These are only the outward, physically obvious things. The damage to my self-esteem, identity, emotions, mind, and soul was even worse.

When I finally acknowledged and addressed what had been done to me, I was able to move past being stuck looking back, I realize how sexual abuse and rape have affected my life and all of my large and small decisions. When I finally acknowledged and addressed what had been done to me, I was able to move past being stuck.

Come along, on the next steps, in this amazing journey!

LABELS ARE UNIMPORTANT

You might say to me what happened to you was not abuse or rape, or that traumatic. That's what I thought about my situation for a very, very long time. What happened to me might not have been right or good, but it wasn't rape and it wasn't that traumatic.

It is not important to label what happened to you. However, you do have to acknowledge it happened. More importantly, you have to admit even though you may not realize it, it has, and still is, affecting your life, even if it happened years ago.

YOU ARE NOT ALONE

I write to let you know you are not alone in your journey. Besides my own personal story, the statistics on sexual trauma and rape are staggering. As you read these numbers, remember these types of offenses are not always reported to the police or other agencies. Due to fear, shame, guilt, lack of family support, and many other issues, a large portion of people do not report these crimes. Therefore, they are not included in the statistics. I am in those hidden numbers.

The Rape, Abuse & Incest National Network (RAINN) (8/15/15) reports how many people over 12 years old are affected by rape.

- 44% of victims are under age 18; …80% of them are under age 30.
- Every 107 seconds, an American is sexually assaulted, 293,000 people per year.
- 17.7 million American women have been victims of rape or attempted rape.

These numbers show you are not alone. You are part of a huge group, almost 18 million people. **You are not alone.**

RAINN also reports girls, ages 16-19, are four times more likely than the general population to be victims of rape or sexual assault. In 2014, according to the Center for Disease Control (CDC), one in four girls and one in six boys are victims of sexual abuse before the age of 18. **You are not alone.**

The research on sexual victimization is similar throughout the world. In 2004, WHO (World Health Organization) reviewed research on sexual victimization in childhood from around the globe and summarized it in Understanding and Addressing Violence against Women - Sexual Violence. They found 27% of girls worldwide have been the victims of sexual assault and 14% of the boys. Some of their studies showed as many as 33.2% of respondent's reporting sexual violence before reaching the age of 18 in sub-Saharan Africa. **You are not alone.**

The numbers show how not alone you are in the world if you have experienced trauma. It is a topic most people will not acknowledge. It is a topic most will ignore. It is a topic some cannot bear hearing about. It is real. It is time to share and let everyone know – **you are not alone in this.**

Although you and the others may not be aware you both share the experience, know there are **more people than you think that share the experience with you.**

AFTER-EFFECTS OF RAPE

RAINN reports the victims of sexual assault are:

- 3 times more likely to suffer from depression
- 6 times more likely to suffer from post-traumatic stress disorder
- 13 times more likely to abuse alcohol
- 26 times more likely to abuse drugs
- 4 times more likely to contemplate suicide.

RAINN provides an estimate of the number of girls that have gotten pregnant as a result of their rape. They estimated in 2012, there were 17,342 possible pregnancies. They believe this number is a high estimate. However, even if one girl was pregnant as the result of rape, that is one girl too many.

STATS ARE NOT THE END…

These statistics are very depressing and very intimidating. This information, combined with my own twisted thoughts and feelings, led me to believe my life was over the second this happened to me.

I am here to tell you, your life is not over.

Let's not stay stuck in the stats.

There are many people you see or hear every day on TV and the radio who have lived through this experience: Oprah, Lady Gaga, Joyce Meyer, and thousands of others have led great lives and are doing great things.

I was able to turn my life around. You can too. You do not need to be a statistic. Trauma leading to these effects does not need to be your final answer in life. There is life after trauma. In fact, there is even **triumph over trauma.**

COME ALONG ON A JOURNEY
OF HOPE AND HEALING

I hope my story will be an inspiration to you to find healing in your life. There are resources, both in this book and online, that can help you to achieve the life you were destined to lead. Sexual trauma does not need to stop you from anything. Come join me on a hope journey– leading to triumph.

Let's go on a journey of hope and healing. Let me share my story with you. I want to make sure you have the support you need as you go through this process. Reading other people's stories can bring back vivid memories and flashbacks that are difficult to deal with. Many times, it is impossible to deal with them without outside help. If you need support, and I would say everyone does at some point in their journey, please see the resource section at the back of the book. It provides excellent resources to get the help you need.

I sincerely wish I could be there for each and every one of you reading this, to help you through your journey. I would like to let you know that I've been there and you will feel better. The strong emotions won't last forever.

I want to let you know it is going to be OK.

I want to let you know that it's not your fault. There are many people who love you whether you are aware of it right now or not. You must know you are loved and accepted.

If you commit to the journey, you can find your life again. You can start getting beyond the consummation of trauma and move onto being YOU. This may be the YOU that you were before, or it may be like me, the YOU that you never got to experience before, because the trauma happened so early in life.

Either way, you are in for a journey that will inspire and encourage you. It will show you a change from the inside out. It will bring you better friendships, family relationships, and all relationships, including the one you have with yourself. You are more than a statistic and you are not alone.

To read more details about the specifics of my assaults, feel free to read the appendix. I did not include details in the regular chapters because the details are graphic and I do not want people to feel that they must read them to get everything out this book. I only include the details in the appendix, so you know I can relate.

The details of the physical assaults unfortunately are only the start of the trauma. The rest of the trauma, which is even more painful, is not as easy to see. I wouldn't realize until much later, how much these events scared me, and not just physically. The physical events were the least of the trauma.

These events stole my life away from me. They stole my body. They stole my mind, memory, and thoughts with fear. They stole my voice- silenced in sadness. They stole my soul – with guilt, shame, and internal anger. They stole any chance at healthy relationships, life choices, and so much more. Because these events started so early in my life, I never really had a chance to have a life to begin with. My life, my innocence, my peace, my happiness, and my everything, was stolen.

At the age of 12, in that bathroom, after being raped, my mind determined it was too late for me. My life was over as I knew it and it would never be the same. I was not good enough. I never would be good enough now. I did not have a story worth sharing or a voice to share it with. My life was left there on that bathroom floor at 12 years old, with that piece of bloody toilet paper.

Looking back from where I am now, the scariest part of the whole thing is I had no idea what was happening to my life. I thought everyone went through this, or at least, everyone felt like this for one reason or another. I thought I was doing a great job of moving on from it.

Keep on moving, that's not affecting me. Do the next right thing. Move on to bigger and better things. Ignore it and it will go away. Really, I was running from it by keeping busy. College, working three jobs, law school, two kids, stressful marriage, successful career, life-threatening illness, separation, divorce, secrets, perfectionism, controlling and pleasing people. It was all to cover the shame, guilt, disgust, and powerlessness that I felt constantly, without even knowing it.

Little did I know, much later, it would all come crashing down. At that breaking point, I would be abandoned, rejected, and alone for so long, I would start screaming,**"I Just Want My Life Back!"**

Chapter 2

MY MIND STOLEN: COVERING IT UP...FEAR

My mind was stolen. First, my memory covered up the events. It was as if they never happened. My little mind and body were thrown into a state of fear, fright, and panic. It stayed there for over 20 years for the earliest events. I was very scared. The terror of the events were so painful and powerful that my mind blocked them out.

My thoughts terrorized me. Living my life was scary. I was constantly waiting for the next event or episode of painful things to happen.

In addition to the terror, I had never had any sex talk at all. I had no file in my brain to put it into, so I just purged out the info (for then). I couldn't label any of this; I didn't even know what it was. For the initial events, I was much too young. The later events did not play out like I thought of rape. When I thought of rape, I thought of a girl walking home late at night and a guy coming out of the alley with a knife and forcing her to have sex. This was definitely not rape. This was my fault.

Secondly, my thoughts went from terror to blaming myself. They shifted from external fear to internal self-hatred. I used control, perfectionism, and other methods to cover up my extreme self-hatred.

Though I was not consciously aware of the events, the events were still very much in control of my life. Fear ruled my mind and my life. I never knew anything other than fear and fighting for my life from toddlerhood on. I never had a life outside of abuse. I had fear of anger, fear of men, fear of disappointment, and fear of not being good enough. I was afraid of everything. Any situation I was in, led me to fear.

FEAR

What should have been external anger was replaced with internal emotions in overdrive. First and foremost was fear–always expecting something bad would happen. I lost courage easily and often. In fact, my fear level would have been at the degree of terror, a painful agitation in the presence or anticipation of danger.

At the age of five and younger, I was impressive of every situation I went into. I always expected something horrible was going to happen. I had already experienced physical abuse at the hands of angry adults. I had already experienced sexual abuse at the hands of very nice, quiet adults. I was threatened and assaulted in many ways before I attended my first day of kindergarten. I had no other way of processing life. I knew nothing other than victimization and abuse. Terror was really the only emotion I felt.

When I look up synonyms for fear, I find many words. These words summarized my entire life. Not one of these words is too strong or too weak. These are words that filled my mind constantly. Not one of these words would not fit the exact profile of my life from birth to 33 years of age. I felt them every single day of my life. In fact, I felt almost all of them daily, if not hourly. It was paralyzing.

Fear was so consuming that it is hard to give examples of it from my life, because EVERYTHING was consumed by it.

One example of fear is rejection. Rejection–not wanted, unsatisfactory, not fulfilling requirements; refusal to believe, accept or consider; not good enough for some purpose; something that cannot be used or accepted. The way that rejection was most evident in my life was in my demeanor.

Starting at the age of five or less, I was extremely shy. I would not talk at all. I was so shy that my kindergarten teacher became concerned. She got the officials involved at some point, although I do not recall this at all. It's obvious that nothing came of it.

After the second event, the shyness got even worse. I went from shy to withdrawn. I would not engage in much of anything. I had one or two friends, but I really pulled away from everything at this time.

The fear, shyness, and isolation got worse as the abuse was repeated. Each time, it took more of a turn for the worse in me. After the second round of abuse (the rape), I withdrew even more from life than I had before. I was more sullen and withdrawn to the point where I would hardly talk. I was so shy that even when I would talk, I would whisper because no one really cared anyway. My appearance went into self-protection mode. My level of trust went from zero to negative-twenty. Everything went from bad to worse. I was imploding, but no one knew. My parents, teachers, and friends did not know. There was no one but me. I was too afraid and didn't have words to attempt to say something.

Another example of fear is abandonment. Abandoned–not adequately guarded or sustained. To cause someone to stop being friendly or helpful; no longer part of a group. A person from those whom loyalty is expected and it stresses the effects of alienation without actual separation. It makes the abandonment work. I was my only source of help and support. I expected loyalty from no one. My parents did not protect me. My friends have also let me down and abandoned me many times. This is true even today with staff and volunteers in my work.

Because I was constantly keeping secrets, I didn't feel like I fit in anywhere. This included school, gymnastics, or anywhere. I could not be real with anyone. To deal with this, I did my best to blend into the wall and look unappealing. If I did not draw attention to myself, no one would notice me. Going unnoticed would be a good thing, because if someone noticed me, bad things would happen. That was demonstrated in my life with angry, raging outbursts as well as the sexual abuse. Quiet blending was the best that I could hope for in life.

There was no time or place for fun in my life. I had to be on constant alert. All of these events took place at fun events, such as holidays and birthday parties. Fun is not fun. Fun is dangerous. Fun is not OK. I would stay out of activities. I always had to be on high alert. Life was not about having fun–it was about protecting yourself from the next horrible situation that would be coming your way. No one was there to protect me, so I needed to be on constant alert status.

There was really not much in me other than fear. It was looming so close, I didn't even see it as fear. I saw it as life. I assumed everyone lived like this.

Though the specific memories of the event were still unconscious, I was exhibiting behaviors that would show my body and mind remembered what happened. This even included the specific words spoken.

The fear manifested itself in my life in various physical ways. At 13 years old, I was having migraine headaches. They were debilitating and came once a month and sometimes once a week. I could not be around any light. The light would pierce my eyes and lead to throbbing temples, which led to vomiting. I could not be around any sound. Things like TV, the radio, a dog barking, or a person's voice all resulted in a throbbing head and vomiting. I would need to lie down in a dark, quiet room and sleep it off.

Where did this come from? I did not get my period until I was 16, so it was not hormonal-related. The migraines were the result of persistent fear and constant stress. At the time, I did not even know I was under constant stress. I thought everyone felt like this. I had no clue anything had happened to me in my conscious mind. It was all still locked below the surface. However, my body was exhibiting signs of it.

MIND ON "PROTECT YOURSELF" CONSTANTLY

Overwhelmed is another word for fear. Overwhelmed means to overpower in thought or feeling or to affect someone very strongly; to cause someone to have too many things to deal with.

In an effort to protect myself from future harm, I did a lot of "thinking." It was obvious no one was going to protect me. If I wanted to be safe, I would need to provide the safety. If I could just stay one step ahead of other people, I could keep myself safe. My mind, therefore, would always be on overdrive, trying to think of all the possible ways things would play out and plan for my safety, protection, or escape.

This led to being constantly overwhelmed. I was always thinking of the bad things that could happen and the need for a plan. I was rigid in my schedule and planning. If plans changed last minute, and I had not thought through everything that could go wrong and I was not prepared, I would be very anxious and a lot of times wouldn't go or would be very agitated. I thought everyone lived like this. I didn't know anything different. I now realize this is part of anxiety and post-traumatic stress disorder.

This also led to over-planning. I would not do anything unless I had all the details up front. In an effort to maintain control over things, I would plan things out in advance. I would pack months before a trip for fear I might forget something and it would be the end of the world. I would have my life planned out years into the future. Once I had a family, if we planned to go to the zoo for the day, I would spend all week planning what to take and how it would go. If my husband wanted to change plans at the last minute and go to the park instead, I would FREAK out. We could not change plans. I was ready for the zoo. I was not ready for the park. I would refuse to go and cause a scene about it–if I had to.

MY THOUGHTS WERE NOT MY OWN

My thoughts about myself were just a tape of what my assailants had said to me. I started playing those same tapes for myself. This made the thoughts even more powerful and worse.

I am always making trouble. I'm always causing problems. I am a problem. I am useless. I am damaged goods, because he told me that I was "useless." No one wanted me.

I tried to conceal my disgusting body… who I was, what he did and what I did were all concealed for no one to know, not even me. I started sleeping in my clothes all the time when I was 13 years old, right after the second event. I would be fully clothed with jeans, bra, and shirt… everything… all the time. I felt this would protect me if I was ever in that situation again. One time he caught me in my night gown. I would now be ready and have all my clothes on all the time.

I would cover myself up with turtlenecks as much as possible. I would wear turtlenecks all the time, even in the summer. I wanted to cover my "useless, too small, disgusting body." However, the reality was nobody wanted me. It was a horrible realization. I was not good enough. I was not worthy of anything or anyone. Life and the fact that this kept happening over and over again confirmed this. At that point in time, with these thoughts replaying in my mind, I realized that I was damaged. Ugly. Not enough. Not good enough.

This is not about him or them. It is about me. In my mind, this trauma wasn't rape. I hardly even told him to stop. This isn't what you see in the movies or hear people tell about rape. Rape happens on the street when it's dark and some guy who you don't know grabs you. That's rape. Since this was a person I knew and trusted, it could not be labeled as rape. Therefore, it must be my fault.

In my head, I plowed ahead in life, carrying the blame of the event on my shoulders. I pretended that it never happened. It definitely was not rape, so it must be my fault.

My mind turned my own intelligence against me. My thoughts turned from *I'm not good enough, useless–to this is all my fault. I deserve this. My own analysis of the situations confirmed this.* I officially took on the guilt and shame. *This is just me being stupid. This is all my fault.*

I must have done something to ask for this.

It's not just one person. Now, it's two. It must be me. It is my fault.

Why wouldn't I have said something?

I felt constant guilt about all of this. Why did I lay there at the time? Why didn't I scream? Why didn't I tell someone? I should have known better than to agree to let him touch me to begin with. If I would have stood up then, then this wouldn't have happened. At the time, why didn't I fight him off more? During the incidents in his bedroom, when I was 14 years old, I didn't even say "stop" or "get off me." Clearly, I deserved this anyway.

IT IS NOT AFFECTING ME

Over the next several years, I believed this trauma was not affecting me. In my mind, it was done and over with and I was moving on. I kept moving. I kept running, running from the fear and the thoughts. I would make my life so busy I wouldn't think of anything.

I was in college, working two or three jobs, going out with friends and dating a few nice people. My life was moving forward and I rarely consciously thought about that event. I was doing well, so I thought. Looking back, I can now see things that led to more problems down the road.

I was always running from one thing to the next. I never would just take some time to relax or just have fun for no other purpose. There was never any time to just sit and be. I didn't know who I was. I was afraid of people finding who I really was and rejecting me. This pattern repeatedly played itself out in my life. It happened with friendships, relationships, school, kids, marriage, work, and non-profit work. In fact, it still happens today.

Stuffing my worry down deep where I wasn't thinking about it – I thought was working really well. I was trying to out-run my vulnerability, fear, feelings of not enough, and uncertainty. I was abandoned, rejected, and alone.

I developed some strategies that actually worked really well. It involved perfectionism and people pleasing no matter what it took. I am what I accomplish. I always sought to earn approval and acceptance. I was always focused on others and what they would think. What would they do?

THOUGHTS LEAD TO WALLS OF PERFECTION TO KEEP ME SAFE

Over the years, without even knowing it, I built up emotional walls in my mind and life to protect me. My first line of offense was to be as close to perfect as possible and to appear perfect to everyone else. I felt if I did that, everyone would like me and I wouldn't be lonely.

My way of getting through life was to act like the perfect person. This included my parents and even my "best friends." I kept them at a distance, so they wouldn't really know me or know I was not perfect. I had a few friends. However, I kept up the perfectionist image so they would accept me. There was no reason not to accept me. I was "perfect." I did not rely on them to help me with my problems and I did everything I could to help them with theirs.

That didn't leave a lot of reasons to reject me, if this was the way I would operate in relationships. It led to me not getting too close to anyone. It gave me protection from having to let them really get to know me. It also gave me ammunition since I really did know them. It was a very safe position. However, my life was paralyzed and I had no idea.

I pretended everything was OK, when it wasn't. What can I do for you? Don't worry about me. I didn't have any other options. I was flying solo in this big world, when it came to my problems. There was nothing that I could do about it. I was abandoned, rejected, and alone.

MEMORIES COME BREAKING THROUGH

All of the behaviors above were in place before I even consciously knew what happened.

My mind kept the memories locked away from my consciousness for awhile. The mind has an amazing way of doing that when we cannot physically do anything about it. For our own emotional protection, the mind blocks out situations. As I got older, things started coming back to the surface of my mind.

Fast forward to my junior year of high school. I'm 16-years-old, soon to be 17. I'm up in my bedroom at the new house my parents built, just hanging out by myself doing homework. I have the television on and I am watching an after-school special movie on Channel 12. They used to have specials on after school, which were two-hour movies about various topics facing middle and high school kids. I remember it vividly, even now 20+ years later.

I was sitting on my desk chair at my built-in desk and the TV was on my dusty blue filing cabinet, not far away. I don't remember much about the movie, except a girl was lying down with a boy on top of her and she was yelling, "It hurts, it hurts. Stop, it hurts. Get off of me." As I was watching the movie, the details of what happened to me years earlier in the second event came flooding back into my mind.

I remembered everything. The touches. The feelings. The pain. The words. The powerlessness. The fear. All of it came crashing over me right there in that room, on that chair. All alone. Sobbing, I just sat there, unable to move.

Everything came flooding back. I didn't know what to do. My life was spinning out of control. The emotions were flowing, but I did not know what to do with them. I had no idea how to handle them. Because of my shyness, isolation, and perfectionism, I did not have a support system of people around me to help me either.

NOWHERE TO GO

So, here it is… my life is in shambles. I have nowhere to go. I don't know what to do. I didn't have anyone to talk to. There I was, after watching this movie, swept to the ground again. I had no one to turn to and nowhere to run. I was all alone, rejected, and abandoned again.

The assailant's words were running through my head:

"No one will believe you."

"You will be in trouble, if someone finds out."

"Don't tell anyone or YOU will be in trouble for being naughty."

I couldn't tell anyone. My mom–not an option. Her possible reactions terrified me. Would she be angry with me? What I feared even more, probably, was that she wouldn't believe me. Or worse yet, that she wouldn't care or do anything about it. Would she blame me, like he said she would, and like I did in my own mind?

My dad was a very quiet and withdrawn person. He was at work all day long. I would not know how to even approach him with anything like this tragedy. And what would he do about it, even if I did?

Church was no place for answers. My mom forced us to go to church and then confirmation classes in the 8th grade. That was definitely not a place to look for answers.

I didn't see any other options. What about teachers, coaches, or others? I lived in isolation and didn't get involved in group settings. I was only useful if I could help. No one came to my mind. My mind was cluttered with survival and "their" thoughts. "It's your fault, no one will believe you."

Looking back now, I can think of one or two people that would have been trustworthy choices—from Girl Scouts connections. My mind was so terrified, confused, and overwhelmed with negative thoughts and uncontrolled emotions that no people came to mind. My thoughts were consumed and overpowered by their words to me.

Instead these thoughts came:

Why would anyone listen? I believed I didn't have a presence in the world without being perfect. If I didn't have something to offer the situation, what is the point of being in conversation with me? Why would they listen, if I had nothing to offer them?

Why would anyone believe me? It had been years since this happened. I had no proof of anything. No one would believe me over him. He had the power and control and I just needed to stay quiet.

Why would anyone care? Why would they care about me? Probably the scariest and saddest thing of all, why would they care what happened to me? I didn't think anyone did or would.

These thoughts were confirmed by evidence in my life. I was convinced there was no one who cared about me enough that I could trust. Four major people in my young life: The older perpetrator of sexual abuse, the younger perpetrator of sexual abuse and rape, and my parents for not knowing and not stepping up to protect me. Not that I had any reason to think they knew about it.

So I kept silent. I continued keeping up the façade of perfection. I did everything I could to protect myself.

These were some of the thoughts running through my mind as I was trying to live a life stolen from me, without any concrete word for what had happened to me. My own mind was one of my own worst enemies. I was abandoned, rejected, and alone.

Though fear was unconsciously controlling my life, my voice being stolen was an even more painful motivator for me to finally shout, **"I Just Want My Life Back!"**

MY VOICE STOLEN:
FROM SADNESS TO SILENCE

My voice was stolen from me. Threats and intimidation silenced me. My own mind silenced me by not remembering the events for awhile. My thoughts and terror silenced me.

This is the hardest part to write. If you lost your voice, what is there to say? Not a lot. It has taken years in the process of writing of this book to fully understand how much my stolen voice has affected me.

My perfectionism also led to an extreme desire to control all situations because of my lack of trust in anyone. That was one of the reasons why my relationships were superficial. If I shared too much, who knows what they would do to me? I just had to keep quiet and be an asset to them. If I did, they would not find out my secrets and reject or abandon me. It was all very exhausting.

In addition to fear–sadness was all over my life. Sadness overwhelmed me as silence filled my life.

A VOICE SILENCED

As a way to start seeing everything taken from me through my silence, I studied the word, voice. Voice comes up in our society mostly when talking about singing. (However, I have absolutely no ability to carry a tune in a song or any other way. I doubt that has anything to do with childhood trauma!)

The level and depth of the voice stolen from me is still affecting me greatly. The effects of my silence are with me every day of my life:

- My inability to formulate words for this experience
- My unspoken words
- My mouth being slammed shut with threats and secrets
- My complete powerlessness
- Being a hollowed-out shell of a person
- My story, not worthy of being heard or written

NO WORDS TO DESCRIBE

Words usually come out of voices. I was so young when this happened I couldn't even formulate words to describe it. It led me into extreme shyness. If I could explain it, what was there to talk about? There was nothing to say. Even if I wanted to, I couldn't stand up for myself. It was impossible. I didn't have words to describe what had happened.

Much later when I did have words to describe it, my internal self-talk blamed myself for the problem. I had nothing to stand up for. I had no identity to stand up for. I was empty. I contained nothing. I lacked meaning, value, or purpose. My words were useless and would just be turned back around and used against me. Even more of a reason to stand silent without a voice was to save myself from further pain.

I was inferior, of poor quality, of little importance, value, or merit. I had been abandoned without needed protection or care when I needed it most. I was alone–separated from others and without any company in my life. Those feelings produced other feelings of bleakness and desolation.

I had nothing to offer, so I would stand silent or, if greatly pressed, whisper. From the fear of having no words to offer the world that mattered, shyness was the outward expression of my silence.

MOUTH SLAMMED SHUT—SECRETS AND HIDING

When thinking further about voice, I thought well, voice comes from your mouth. For me, my mouth was slammed shut. I had to keep the secrets. I thought no one would believe me if I told them. I needed to keep it all secret. People would think badly of me if they knew.

I couldn't control the power and rage that would come at me if I didn't keep my mouth shut. It was just safer to keep my mouth closed. Keep the secrets. At least I knew what life was like if I kept the secrets. The fear of the unknown was so much scarier to me than the known. I did just that for over 17 years. I never told one soul on this earth what had happened to me.

If I told anyone, it wouldn't go well for me. It would bring me right back into the abandonment, despair, guilt, shame, and fear. The easiest thing to do was just keep silent. I was absolutely sure it was best to keep my mouth shut and keep the secrets well hidden from everyone and even myself forever.

I had no personality and no character of my own. My only personality was "What can I do to help you have a better life?" The problem was I had no identity of my own. I was completely empty inside. I had no story of my own to share. I was only present in the world to help other people. I was not needed for fun or any reason at all. I only was wanted when I could help someone. This perception drove me into a persistent life of servanthood and devotion to listening.

NO VOICE = POWERLESSNESS

Martin Luther King, Jr. defined power as "The ability to effect change." In my digging for the definition of voice, I found some interesting words. Merriam Webster has many definitions for voice. The two that stood out the most for me are:

- The power or ability to produce …tones;
- The right of expression; also : influential power.

I don't normally associate voice with power. However, it makes total sense. To get a sound, you need to use power through your vocal cords to make them vibrate and produce the sound. We need to voice/express our concerns to make sure they are known and addressed. Whether we like how they are addressed or not is another issue. However, we need to make them known, so they can be addressed.

I had a total loss of hope. My only focus was on controlling my safety. Even that wasn't going well. My powerlessness and my inability to influence or produce an effect were apparent. The same was true of my insufficiency and my lack of adequate power, capacity, and competence.

It was obvious why I could not produce any voice in my life. I had no power. I was powerless, because my voice was muted. The little I had left, I used to protect myself. I didn't matter. My voice didn't need to be heard. I expressed this emptiness in shyness.

My power was taken from me physically. In the early abuse, my hands were held above my head and someone was sitting on my chest to squeeze the voice out of me. Therefore, I could not scream for help. I had no power over my body. I released this power to anyone in the room who asked for it. All of the time, there was sheer terror of what they would do to me, if I didn't.

Emotionally, I had no power. I was steamrolled over by another person's rage and anger at an early age. That held me down in fear. I was powerless to do anything about it.

Intellectually, I had no power. In the beginning, I was too young and didn't even have words for these things. Once I was old enough to know the words, I wasn't brave enough to say anything. I wasn't strong enough to stop it.

Spiritually, I was less than powerless. I was left in a heap alone on the ground. I was disgusting, not good enough, and bad–just like they all said. I was in complete isolation and had no one to trust. God was someone I would have to face at my death. He would weigh my bad and good decisions and decide if I deserved heaven. He was of no value here or in any day-to-day life decisions.

My life experience, mind, and body showed me that I had no power and, therefore, I had no voice.

NO IDENTITY
MY VOICE: USE TO PROTECT OTHERS

At the age of 12, after being raped, in that bathroom, my mind determined it was too late for me. My life was over as I knew it and it would never be the same. I was not good enough. I never would be good enough now. I did not have a story worth sharing or a voice to share it with. My life was left there on that bathroom floor at 12-years-old with the piece of bloody toilet paper.

But, instead of going down the depression/suicidal path, my mind led me in another direction. It was toward achievements and proving my worth.

With no identity of my own, this incident made me who I was. My first rule in life was to keep myself safe through my constant thoughts of fear and anxiety.

My second rule of life was to "Protect other kids." I wanted to do everything possible to keep other little kids safe. Hopefully, through my help, they wouldn't have to suffer like I did.

That role felt very comfortable to me on many levels. At any family events, I would hang out with the younger kids. I knew the younger kids wouldn't hurt me. I just didn't want that to happen again, ever. That provided me with protection and safety. I could also protect them from him and others like him. That strategy worked well for quite a while, but it also became, and still is, a destructive pattern in my life.

These two rules I would adopt for the rest of my life: protecting and saving everyone. It was always to my detriment. It led to huge problems in friendships and relationships and is still, today, a stressor for me in relationships.

GUILT

Another expression of sadness for me was guilt. It was internal emotion that overtook me and swept the real me away. Merriam-Webster defines guilt as: "feelings of culpability, especially for imagined offenses or from a sense of inadequacy."

Most of my guilt came from feelings and imagined offenses due to my sense of inadequacy. I was told by my attackers I had done something very wrong. They told me I needed to keep it a secret or I would be in a lot of trouble. I was bad. I had to be careful what I said, so it was best to say nothing. Because of that, I felt guilty all of the time.

I felt guilty that everything I did was wrong. I felt guilty that I was wrong, wasn't good enough, was a bother to people and I wasn't perfect. If I made a small mistake, I had better make up for that mistake. I couldn't even do that. I was forever in debt to the person. This showed up in finances.

One example of the connection between perfectionism and personal guilt occurred when I was in elementary school. When I was in the 5th grade, I rode my brother's bike to the book fair at school which was only a half block from our house. When I left with all my books, I completely forgot the bike and just walked home.

A few days later, my brother was looking for his bike and couldn't find it. My mom asked me about it. I lied and said I had no idea where it was. I then went to the school and looked everywhere, trying to find the bike. However, I didn't find it. I tried to make it right, but it was impossible. A few days later, we found it hanging from the basketball hoop at school with a bent rim.

I felt incredibly guilty for two reasons. First, I was not perfect. I forgot the bike. How could I forget the bike? I knew better than that. How stupid do you have to be to forget the bike you rode there on? Second, I felt guilty because my brother got in trouble for it. I was too afraid to admit my part in it. Anger was so scary to me that I couldn't even think about sharing my part in the problem. Instead, I let my brother take the fall for it, which caused me great guilt.

Once my mind realized the full extent of the trauma and everything that happened, I felt guilty. All of these assaults happened. Therefore, it must be my fault. If this many things happened to me, I must be the problem. It would not have happened this many times unless I did something to ask for it or encourage it. It cannot be their fault, I had something to do with it. This was guilt.

FINALLY, COURAGE TO USE MY VOICE—REACHING OUT

From the first event through the first 17 years of my life, I did not tell anyone about what had happened to me. In fact, I was not even aware of most of what had happened to me. However, finally, like a turtle coming out of a shell (not voluntarily but because of a traumatic run-in), I attempted to reach out to someone and voice what happened to me.

A few months after the experience in my room with the after school special (when the memories had resurfaced of the rape and abuse), something happened. The memories bubbled up again, but this time I was not alone.

I remember arriving at a high school party, ready to have a good time. My friend and I had gotten together to get ready for the party and finally we were on our way. We made our way to the driveway of the house party in my red Ford Escort. We exited the car and were hanging-out outside. Everyone was having a good time.

An hour or so into the party, I was standing by the car talking with some people. I looked up toward the door to the house and there he was. There was a person at the party who looked and had mannerisms just like my assailant.

I lost it. I couldn't function. At first, I was frozen. Finally, after a few minutes, I pulled myself together enough to leave my car and find my friend. Unfortunately, in the process, I had to pass him to go inside.

It took everything I had to do that. In fact, thinking about it now, I am surprised I found the courage. My guess is I was in such a blackout type stage of fear that I didn't even fully know what I was doing. Instead, I was focusing solely on the mission. All I wanted to do was to get her and get out of there. I found my friend inside and told her we had to leave immediately.

My friend was not happy. She had just started drinking and was having a great time. She wanted to stay. Because I was totally controlled by other people's emotions and a sense of over-responsibility, I could not leave her at this party alone. I could not leave without her. Therefore, instead of just telling her I was leaving and then going, I opened the whole situation right there at the party while she was getting drunk. I told her what had happened to me.

I finally opened up to someone about what had happened to me. It took me years, but I did it. I didn't go into all the details. I told her I was raped by someone and this guy at the party was creeping me out. He looked just like the guy and I needed to get out of there.

As I said, she had been drinking. She was only 16 or 17 years old like me. She was not an ideal candidate to tell, and that was not the time to tell her. But, nonetheless, she was the first person I told. After years of silence, I finally broke the silence. I told someone. I told someone about this horrible experience. I let someone in to help me. I did it!

To say that it did not go well would be an understatement.

My friend and I ended up in a yelling and screaming match. I don't even know what we were yelling and screaming about. I remember I ended up sitting back in the car. I sat there crying and crying.

I finally reached out for help. I let someone in. It was someone who was supposed to be my best friend. Instead of empathy, help, or respect, I was abandoned, rejected, and alone again. It was first by him and now by her because of it.

A few people at the party attempted to comfort me. However, the pain of the trauma being revealed, so unexpectedly, combined with being rejected by someone who I thought was my best friend, was just too much. I wasn't even listening to the people. I was hysterical. I did not tell them anything. I couldn't even speak.

I don't remember the rest of the night. I don't even remember leaving or when that finally occurred. However, what I do remember kept me silent for many, many more years. I remember being left to deal with the situation alone again. I felt rejected and abandoned again, just like the day it happened so many years before. It was just like the day the memories came back. I was abandoned, rejected, and alone again.

She was the first and last person I told. I really didn't need to feel that rejection again. I got it loud and clear the first two times. I didn't want that to happen again—EVER! I was silenced again…

It would be over 13 more years before I reached out to anyone else to talk about it. However, much more of life would intercede in the meantime.

UNCONSCIOUS LIFE CHOICES, IT'S NOT AFFECTING ME

I went through my high school years wanting to work in daycare. I could protect the kids. Owning a daycare was my calling. Keeping kids safe was my passion. Through the urging of many friends and a guidance counselor, I was encouraged to apply to college because my parents were going to pay for it.

At first, UW-Whitewater would not accept me. I had taken too many cooking classes and not enough science and math. My guidance counselor, Mr. Becker, called and got me in after some lengthy discussions. After being accepted to college, I started studying early childhood education, the path to my life goal of protecting kids. I would later expand on that and major in child psychology, with a minor in criminal justice and social work.

Other than math, I did well in school. I found it was easy for me. I got A's and B's without studying much. I showed up to every class, took notes and got by. However, I got D's and F's in math which brought me down to a 2.73 GPA.

In the meantime, my parents were legally divorced, not a walk in the park. I lost my car and my offer of payment for college disappeared after the first semester.

NOT AGAIN: ANOTHER EVENT

During college, I worked for a lawyer in a small office downtown. I was about 19-years-old and a sophomore in college. My boss was in his forties or fifties.

I had worked my way up from receptionist to legal secretary/office manager in a matter of months, with no previous experience. I really enjoyed the work and was good at it.

I had been working at this office for a while, but over the last few weeks at the office, the boss had asked me to possibly do some things with him for the office on the weekend. For example, we needed art for the walls in the office and there was an art fair coming up. He asked if I would go with him.

I was uncomfortable with something about the request. However, I felt I had no control over my life and didn't want to be abandoned, rejected, and alone again so, I reluctantly said, "Yes."

With the type of law practiced at this office, we sometimes had appointments on Saturday mornings. Shortly after this request from my boss, there was one particular Saturday morning where it was just me and the lawyer in the office.

The last client had just left. I was changing the toner/drum in the printer. In those days, they recommended you turn down the lights when you changed the printer toner/drum. I pulled the cartridge box out and put it on the counter. I then walked around to turn down the lights. I returned to the counter where the box was located. I started to cut the cartridge out of the silver sealed packaging that it came in. However, before I could even get my hands on the cartridge, he was standing right there in front of me.

I thought he was back in his office to clean up and get ready to leave. I don't know where he came from. It scared me. I had a "startled reflex" response and jumped. He grabbed my shoulders, as if to calm me down.

That scared me even more. Because my body had been stolen long ago, whenever anyone touched me I felt like I had to submit to them. The fact that he touched me threw me off even more.

But then, he pulled me close to him and attempted to kiss me. Somehow, I pulled myself together enough to pull back away from him. I turned toward the cartridge and started cutting open the silver packaging and putting the toner/drum into the printer. I carried on as if nothing had happened. I put the toner into the printer, grabbed my coat and left.

I never said a word about it to anyone. In fact, I've never told this story to anyone until this book. I did go back to the job for a few more weeks, but then just stopped showing up.

Never another word about it.

Abandoned, rejected, and alone. Silenced yet again...

My voice was stolen from me and I was left abandoned, rejected, alone, and silent. However, my soul being stolen was even worse and left me screaming, **"I Just Want My Life Back!"**

MY SOUL STOLEN: SHAME AND ANGER

My soul was stolen from me. My mind, will, and emotions were also all stolen. I talked about my mind being stolen, as well as my memory of the event and my thoughts. My emotions and will were also stolen.

Because my abuse occurred at such an early age, my emotions remained at a toddler level. At the time of my first assaults, I shut my feelings down on a conscious level. I was emotionally numb. It was actually a blessing to not feel anything. Just being was hard enough. I didn't know what to do with any emotions. I didn't know how to act with them. They could not be controlled and I needed everything controlled. If I allowed my own emotions to flow, I would be hurt again.

For the most part, the only feelings I felt were negative-type emotions. I didn't have labels for them. Fear was constant in my life. I did nothing and didn't live a moment without terror of what might happen to me next. It included fear of the unknown, fear of the known, fear of other people's emotions, and especially angry outbursts. It was constant, overwhelming fear.

Happiness was very fleeting and passing. That is not to say there were not moments in my life where I experienced some happiness. We traveled a lot as a family. Going together on trips was fun. There were moments of happiness. Something good would happen at school or in an activity and I was happy and proud. Those moments were few and far between. At times, I would feel happy in a singular moment with friends. However, the fear and anxiety would loom all the time and still does today when good things happen.

My normal state of mind was on constant alert for danger and to feel ashamed for whom I was. This message was reinforced in what I was hearing at church in confirmation classes. If I was "good enough" on my death (did more good things than bad things), Jesus would decide if I could come into heaven. In my mind, God really hated me and all that was in me. I was not good enough for him and never could be, unless I did enough good things.

I learned this is not an accurate description of God, but this is what I heard at the time.

Why were emotions so overwhelming and dangerous to me?

At best, my emotions would be passed to me by other people. I saw any emotion as something someone else caused me to feel. My emotions were imposed on me by other people. I could not feel anything without someone else causing me to. To feel good, someone had to appreciate me, so I had to help someone. To feel sad, someone would have to say or do something to me. I did not have my own conscious feelings or emotions that I had any control over. All of my emotional power was controlled by the hands of whoever I was with.

My research on this matter has shown me that my emotions, other than fear, took on less traditional labels.

- **Sadness**–The pain and sadness went so deep, it wasn't even sadness. It was a normal state.
- **Guilt**–of not living up to people's standards. I disguised the guilt with perfectionism and keeping my distance. Guilt is a feeling of **"I did something bad."** In my life, it went much deeper. It had festered to the point of shame.
- **Shame**–is not living up to your own standards. Life became **"I am bad."** Shame took up permanent and complete residence in my mind and thoughts. It turned my world from "they are against me" to "my own mind is against me."
- **Anger**–took the form of distance, withdrawal, and anxiety.

These emotions were so strong that they became my identity. It changed who I thought I was. *I am bad. I am wrong.*

ANGER

The emotion I remember being exposed to over and over again in my childhood was anger. I was never angry. I was afraid of anger because when adults got angry, bad things would happen to me. This was deeply ingrained in me. These events terrified me when it came to people being angry.

TRADITIONAL ANGER

I wish I could say I was angry in the traditional sense of the word. However, this would not be entirely accurate. My anger was, in fact, stolen. Because the abuse was very early and traumatic, I was intensely afraid of anger.

Looking back now, I wish I would have been angry at my attackers. Instead, I feared them and fear led me right into their hands. I turned all the anger back on myself into guilt, shame, fear, distance, and withdrawal. I did not know anything else. I wish I would have been mad at my parents for not having the "birds and the bees" talk at a young age-appropriate time. Yes, research shows learning proper names for body parts is an ongoing process that can be started at age 2 if you start where a child's curiosity leads. Why didn't my parents tell me what I needed to know before age 5? I wish anger was an emotion that I knew how to handle or at least was not afraid of when I was younger, but it wasn't. Anger was stolen from me even before these incidents. However, these incidents made the danger of anger even more real to me.

My extreme fear of anger led to many problems. First, it led me to avoid getting angry with anyone and also to isolate myself from anyone that might get angry. This left me abandoned, rejected, and alone again.

ANGER AVOIDANCE–FIX EVERYTHING

To protect myself, I would keep the peace at all costs. If it meant lying or withholding information, so be it.

I HAD TO figure out a way to fix situations to avoid someone getting angry about anything. Even if it was not a situation I was directly involved in, I took the weight of the world on my shoulders. I didn't want to get caught in the crossfire of ANYONE'S anger, so I had to fix it. That, in and of itself, was exhausting on top of all my other coping mechanisms, but it was all I could do to stay safe.

This was true even at the age of four or five. If I could just find the thing that person needed, they wouldn't be mad and hit me. I could just be better at finding things. If J and K were arguing about a ball on the playground, I would seek out another ball for them to play with so they wouldn't have to fight about it. I would fix it. I would fix everything. It was not a choice–I HAD TO. The fear was that strong.

An example is a group project where no one wanted to do part Y. The silence would kill me, so I would step up and do that part. This is true even if I was also doing parts A, B, C, and D. I would also take on that part so no one would get into any conflict about it. I still do this much of the time. I don't like that silence and I will jump in and save the day! It is a detrimental oddity in family life and reaching your personal goals and dreams.

If someone would raise their voice, I would tremble. If I knew I would disappoint someone, I would become extremely fearful and stressed. I was fearful that the anger would come out at me and I would be hurt physically, emotionally, or both. I had the primitive feeling of fight or flight constantly, like the feeling you get before a bad car accident, where you brace yourself before the big crash.

My avoidance of anger was so intense that it went a step further. If a situation between two other people was starting to escalate and it looked like there could be conflict, it was my job to defuse conflict so no one would get hurt. It might mean I would agree to do something I might not want to do, just so the situation would go away. It could also mean I would think up something to defuse the situation, which may or may not have been true. Then, I would go about making that statement true to the best of my ability because I didn't want to be known as a liar. Actually, to say the weight of the world was on my shoulders would be an understatement. This burden was a tall order, especially for a 5-year-old.

This tactic was especially true with adults. The adults needed to know that I had everything under control so they would not fly off the handle. "They" could not be trusted. Anger could develop at any time with consequences to me. So unless I had guaranteed good news, I would not share anything. I had to keep bad news to myself and figure out a solution myself that would guarantee no anger would erupt. This had the effect of increasing my abandonment, rejection, and isolation.

In addition to the pure fear of anger, I didn't want to be angry because I didn't want to be out of control and hurt anyone. If I stuffed the feeling of anger deep away, then no one, including me, would be endangered. I would take the edge off stifled emotions by ignoring them. When that didn't work, I would blame myself and keep myself busy so I wouldn't realize them. I would continue the perfectionist appearance, and if all that failed, I would go shopping.

As a result, I suffered terrible physical and emotional consequences throughout my childhood and well into my adult life. I stayed in unhealthy situations so I didn't rock the boat for anyone else, even when I was suffering and miserable. The result was **migraines, strep throat, abusive relationships, broken hearts, no boundaries, and over-responsibility.** I was afraid someone would be mad, so I just stayed and remained silent.

ANGER = PEOPLE-PLEASING
Do Everything, Help Everyone, Over-Responsibility

The fear of anger led to constant people pleasing throughout my life. I couldn't do anything without everyone around me agreeing it was a good idea. I had no ideas or thoughts for myself about whether something was a good idea or not. I would ask my friends or family what to do. If I asked them, then I had to do what they said or I would be disappointing them. I always felt trapped. I literally could not make decisions on my own most of the time. I needed someone else's feedback. However, once I got that feedback, even if I didn't want to, I was forced into accepting their opinion so I would not upset them.

When I looked at synonyms for the word *"anger"*, I found the words: mad, hateful, threatened, hurt, aggressive, frustrated, distant, critical, embarrassed, devastated, jealous, resentful, violated, furious, enraged, provoked, hostile, infuriated, irritated, withdrawn, suspicious, skeptical, and sarcastic. When I look at these words, I can relate to about half of them. However, I would not have labeled myself as angry because of my extreme fear of it.

I was embarrassed by who I was. I was also devastated by how I dealt with what had been done to me. Initially, I was threatened by the perpetrators. Then, I felt threatened in almost every situation presented to me afterwards. I was hurt by my parents through no fault of theirs and many others. Later in life, I had great frustration. I was always distant. I was withdrawn, shy, fearful, and definitely lived in isolation. That was how anger reared its nasty head. It was definitely controlling my life.

SHAME

I did not feel a lot of sadness, in the traditional sense of the word, while I was growing up. I was not crying or feeling "sad." However, when I look up synonyms for *"sad"* I find the words abandoned, ashamed, despair, depressed, lonely, bored, empty, isolated, indifferent, inferior, vulnerable, powerless, victimized, ignored, and guilty. I can relate again to each and every one of these words. If you asked me to list words about myself, these would be the words I would use to describe me. This was the sum-total of who I was and who I thought I would always be.

An internal emotion that went into overdrive was shame. *Shame* takes away part of us that believes we can change and be better. Over and over again, I thought, "I am never good enough."

- I am inferior in everything.
- I am stupid.
- I am not good enough.
- I am ashamed of my decisions.
- I am ashamed of my body. I was very sickly-looking and skinny while I was growing up. I was made fun of at school. In fact, I remember that in 3rd grade they called me blubber butt (ironic considering I was skinnier than a rail). It hurt me greatly. Not only did my family reject me, but the kids at school were now doing the same thing. There was no safe place anymore.
- I was ashamed I was alive.
- I wished I had never been born. I felt hopelessness daily and most often hourly.

LEADING TO MORE SECRETS AND HIDING

I was ashamed of my thoughts. I needed to keep them hidden. I had to keep my secrets to myself so no one else would know. It would cause me more pain if people knew, so I watched everything I said and what others were saying. However, I was barely conscious I was even keeping a secret at the time. The effort of keeping these secrets caused me more distress and anxiety than I realized.

I could keep track of my story if I had only had one person to tell it to. Most of my life, I had only one or two friends at a time. Those relationships were more about them and not much at all about me. Besides, no one wanted to know anything about me. No one cared what I thought or wanted. I was just a pawn for people to use as they wanted. I was left to deal with the fall-out in silence and alone.

PRODUCED MORE FEAR, BLAME, AND ISOLATION

I was to blame for all of this mess. It all started when I said nothing and agreed to playing doctor. Therefore, I figured I must have asked for it. I viewed myself as tainted goods. I thought everyone could tell I was sexually abused and raped. This was going to happen over and over again. It had already happened over and over again. I felt that I must have been asking for it. I reasoned that, in my case, it really wasn't trauma or rape because I let him touch me in the first place. I didn't tell him to stop. I should have known better. I should have told someone. I should have done something different. It shouldn't have felt "good." It was all my fault.

Isolation. It kept me so shy. I felt unworthy and it kept me distant from everyone. Hiding secrets didn't help me with social connections. A modern day example: I hosted a shoe drive to collect shoes and money for the work that we do. At the beginning of the drive, I understood we could take ANY shoes, regardless of their condition. Throughout the drive, the rules changed so they only wanted slightly used shoes. I did not share or specify slightly used shoes. I allowed all of the shoes to come in and sorted through them myself to get rid of the ones that wouldn't work. It caused more work for me and my family. It also wasn't totally honest with the people who were participating. However, to avoid conflict or possibly having someone become angry, I didn't do anything about it.

NO IDENTITY—NO WILL OF MY OWN

My will was stolen as well. Will is defined as a strong desire and determination. I had no will of my own.

I am not good enough. I will never be good enough, no matter what I do or don't do. It led me down a road of not having any likes or dislikes of my own. I was a chameleon responding to other people's likes and dislikes, so as not to cause trouble. I just took on what the people around me wanted or needed.

I had no idea who I was. My freedom and innocence were stolen long before I could develop likes and dislikes.

I just always went with the flow. I didn't know anything else.

However, because of this, I had no story of my own. I was pretending. My imagination ran wild. I would pretend to have feelings. I would pretend to know what I wanted. I would pretend to have a boyfriend and imagine what it would be like. I would pretend to be a lot of different things.

The best way I can describe it is that I felt like a paper doll. You could cut me, color me, make me into whatever you wanted me to be and if you left me, I would fall to the ground, to be forgotten forever. Empty. Worthless. No backbone to stand up.

If someone didn't like me, I would just be thrown away. I was fun as long as they wanted to play. They could fill me up and out, however they wanted to, but they had all of the control. I was just along for the ride, as long as they would allow me to be.

Until they left me abandoned, rejected, and alone, yet again.

POST-TRAUMATIC STRESS DISORDER

I now understand my emotions were affected by what they call post-traumatic stress disorder (PTSD). Looking at the symptoms of post-traumatic stress disorder brings my life into a lot more order. I wish I would have known about it when I was 17 or 18 and first experienced all this craziness and I didn't know what to do with all of it.

I now realize this was one part of post-traumatic stress disorder. It is what military veterans and other people suffer from when they return from war or other extremely traumatic situations. Once you get closer to safety, physically, your mind starts processing the full extent of the danger you were in and caves in on you in a variety of different ways.

Mayo Clinic defines PTSD as a mental health condition triggered by a terrifying event—either experiencing it or witnessing it. Symptoms may include flashbacks, nightmares and severe anxiety, as well as uncontrollable thoughts about the event. If you are experiencing these symptoms, you need to reach out to a professional counselor for help to get past them.

Looking at the symptoms, as outlined by the Mayo Clinic, I fit almost every one. They arrange the symptoms by groups as outlined below:

Symptoms of **intrusive** memories may include:

- Recurrent, unwanted distressing memories of the traumatic event
- Reliving the traumatic event as if it were happening again (flashbacks)
- Upsetting dreams about the traumatic event
- Severe emotional distress or physical reactions to something that reminds you of the event.

Symptoms of avoidance may include:

- Trying to avoid thinking or talking about the traumatic event
- Avoiding places, activities or people which remind you of the traumatic event.

Symptoms of **negative changes in thinking and mood** may include:

- Negative feelings about yourself or other people
- Inability to experience positive emotions
- Feeling emotionally numb
- Lack of interest in activities you once enjoyed
- Hopelessness about the future
- Memory problems, including not remembering important aspects of the traumatic event
- Difficulty maintaining close relationships.

Symptoms of changes in **emotional reactions** may include:

- Irritability, angry outbursts or aggressive behavior
- Always being on guard for danger
- Overwhelming guilt or shame
- Self-destructive behavior, such as drinking too much or driving too fast
- Trouble concentrating
- Trouble sleeping
- Being easily startled or frightened

If you feel these symptoms describe you, please search for help. You will not be able to get through this trauma on your own. You may need to be in therapy the rest of your life, but you will need help. I was in therapy for about a year and I was dealing with a divorce, a near-death experience, as well as childhood trauma. Do not try to think you can blow through this experience on your own. You will not be able to. Please reach out for the help of a doctor/ psychologist. There are resources at the back of this book. Some of them are free, while others have a fee.

I was constantly being blown back and forth in storms caused by other people's emotions. Other people's emotions, which I, of course, had absolutely no control over. It was a scary place to be and I didn't know anything different. All of this mess led me to make really poor decisions in relationships and in life. It left me wondering what life I even had left to get back. However, I was abandoned, rejected, and alone, again and again.

Probably of all the things stolen from me, my emotions were what left me most wounded and wanting to scream, **"I Just Want My Life Back!"** I had no control over even myself, let alone my world. All I wanted was a little control.

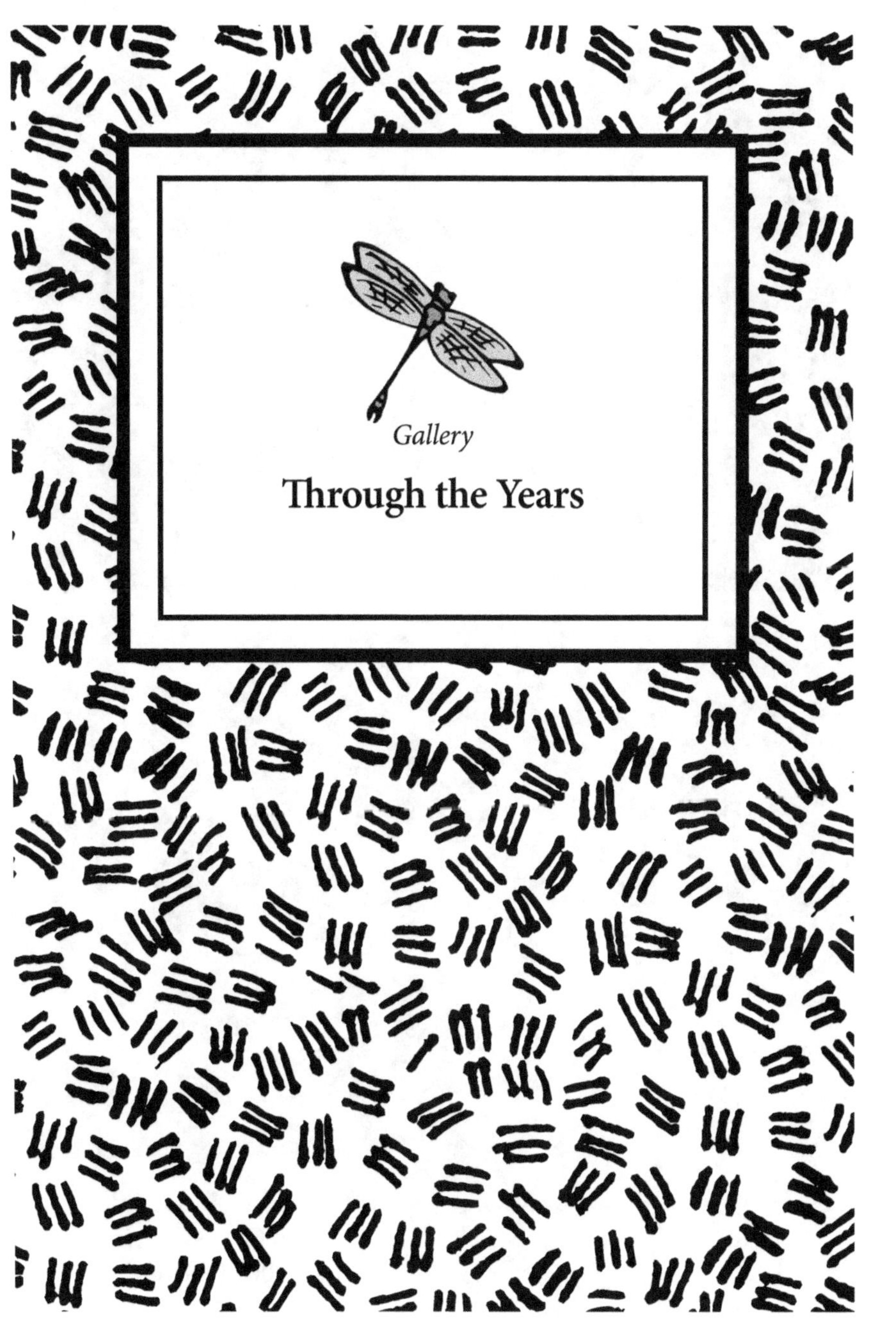

Gallery

Through the Years

On a swing in 1976 (left)
and On a swing in
2004 (above).

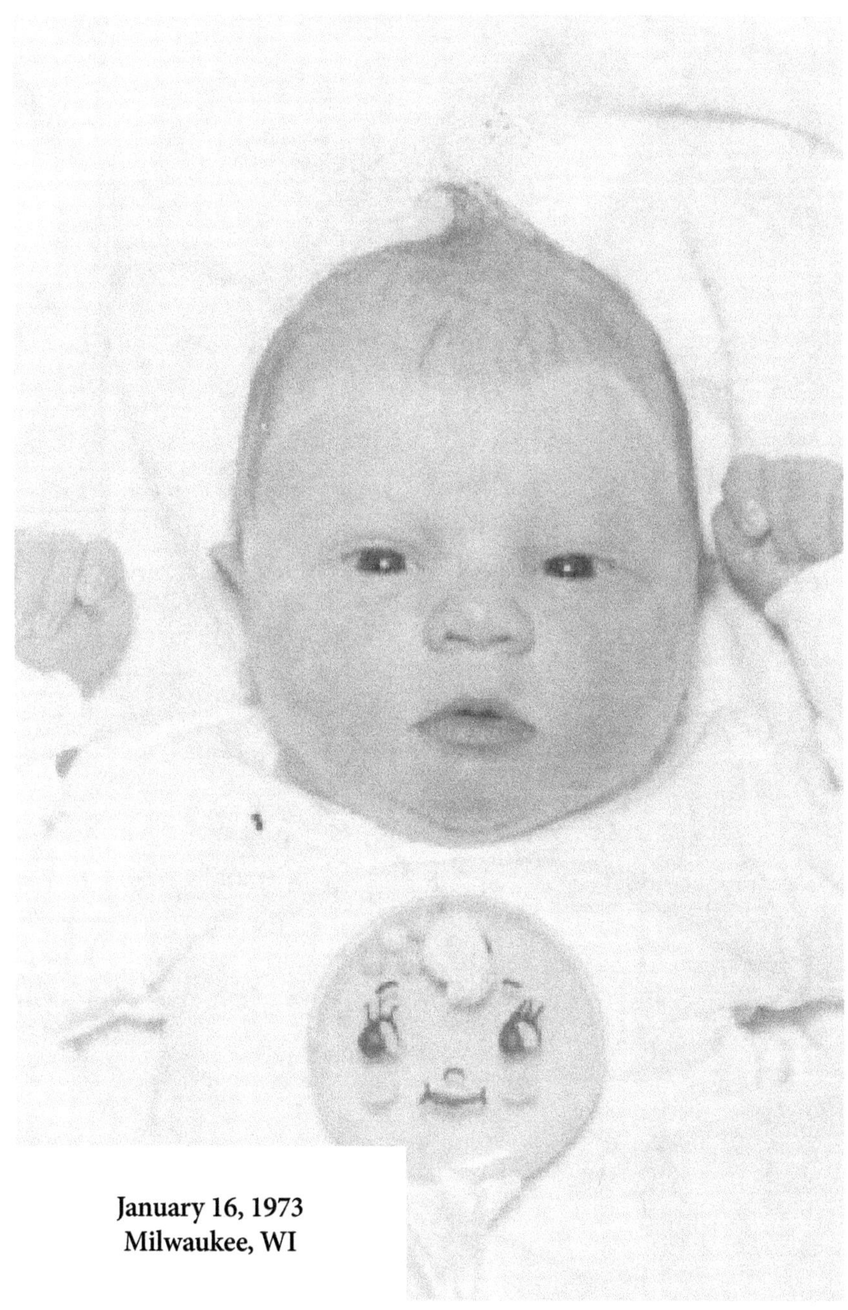

January 16, 1973
Milwaukee, WI

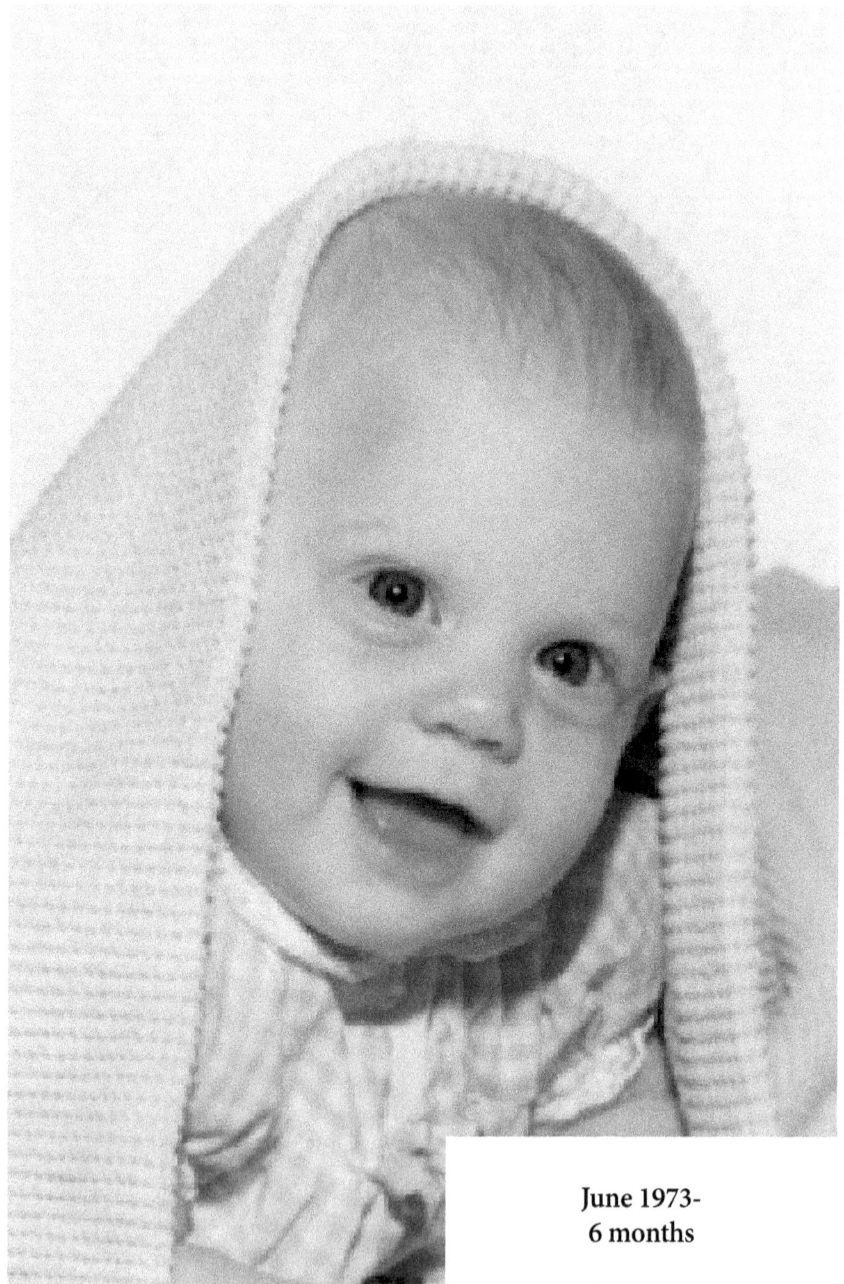

**June 1973-
6 months**

January 1974-
1 year

October 1973 -
Disney World (above)

December 1973 -
Christmas(left)

December 1973-
Christmas (right)

April 1974 -
Popsicle Time (above)

May 1974 -
Helping with laundry (top)

Summer 1974
Loving the wagon!

September 1974

February 1975
2 years old

February 1975
2 years old

1976
Fearful of Santa

1977
Preschool
(4 years old)

1977
Preschool Christmas Pageant
(4 years old)

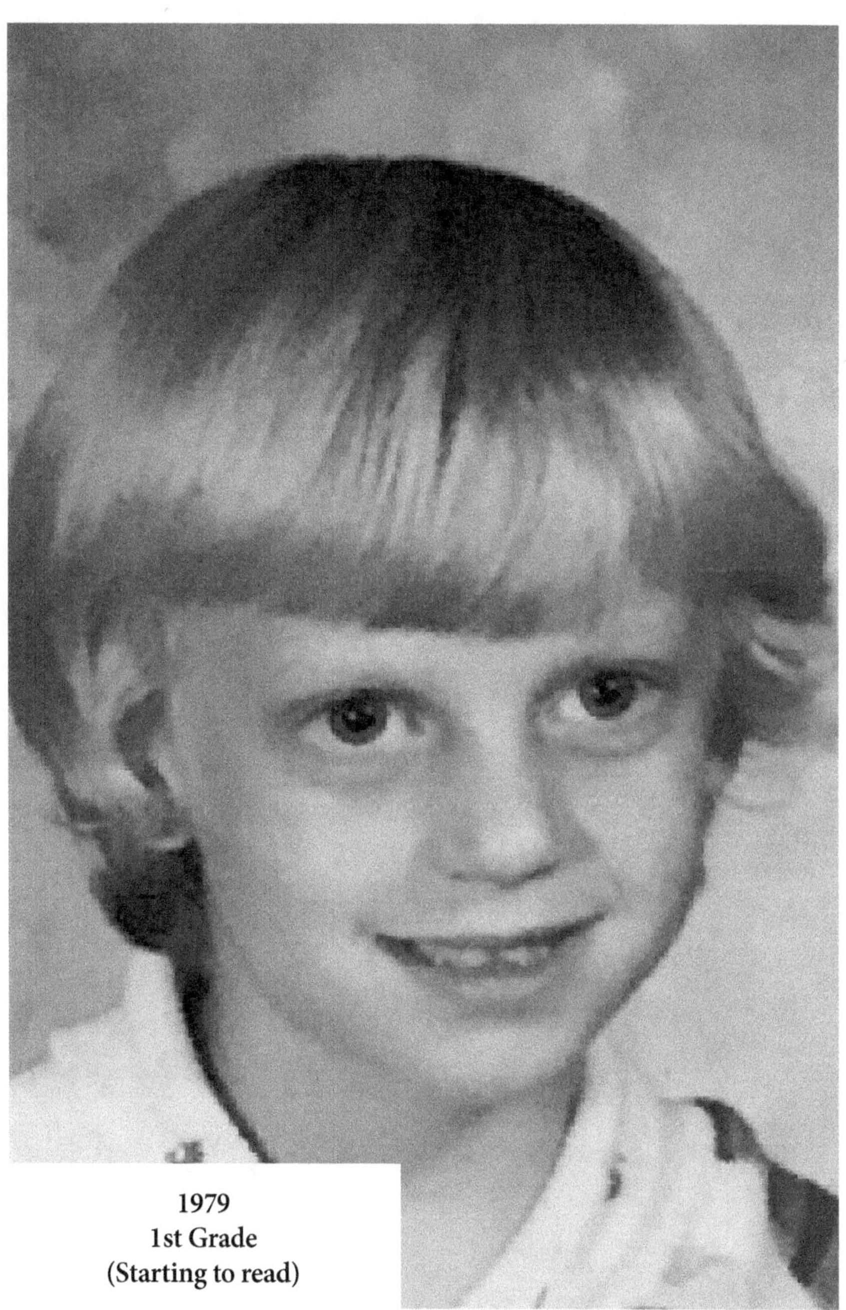

1979
1st Grade
(Starting to read)

1980-1981
2nd Grade
7-8 years old,
(Cursive writing, purple ditto
sheets, Girl Scouts)

**1981-1982
3rd Grade
(Extremely shy)**

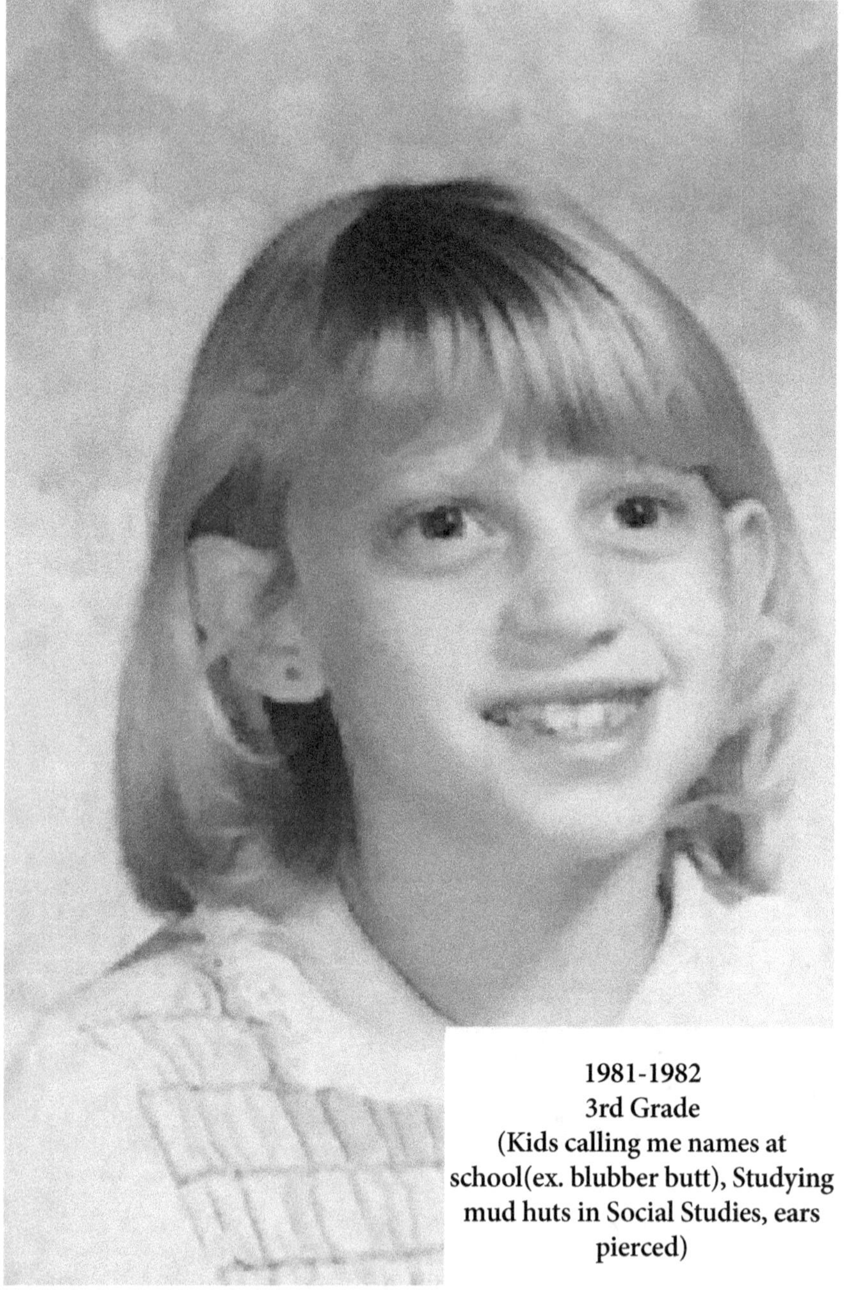

1981-1982
3rd Grade
(Kids calling me names at
school(ex. blubber butt), Studying
mud huts in Social Studies, ears
pierced)

1981-1982
3rd Grade
(I remember this Girl Scout
overnight field trip-I forgot my
PJ's and was devastated.)

Florida Trips With Family

1982 - Daytona Beach
(left)

1983 - First airplane ride
(I was convinced that the plane
would be hijacked by terrorists.)
(above)

1982-1983
4th Grade

Mrs. Philbert was my favorite teacher. We had animals in our room.

Beginning Of the end. The rape happened shortly after this.

1984
Before a recital. Gymnastics was a
huge part of my life.

1985
I loved Annie!

**1985-1986
7th Grade**

**I always wanted a cat and finally
got one, Mischief.**

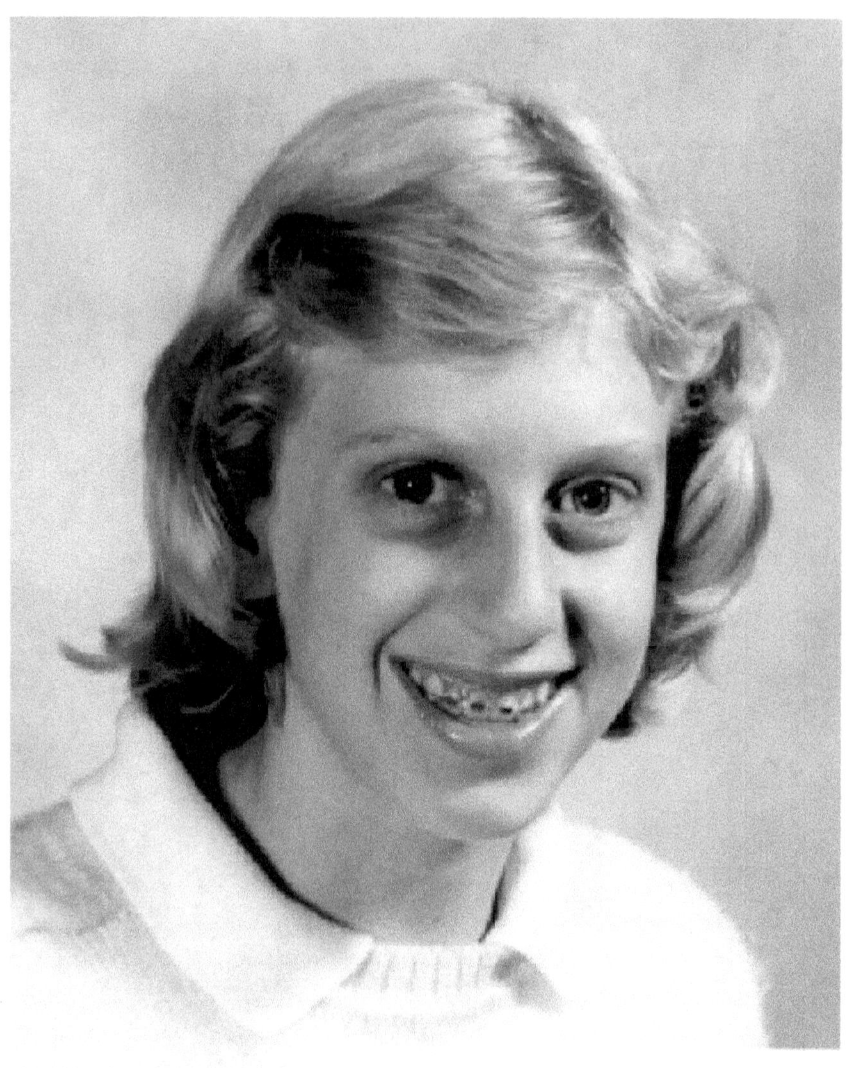

1985-1986
7th Grade

Gymnastics, Junior Achievement,
Home Ec/Shop class, Violin

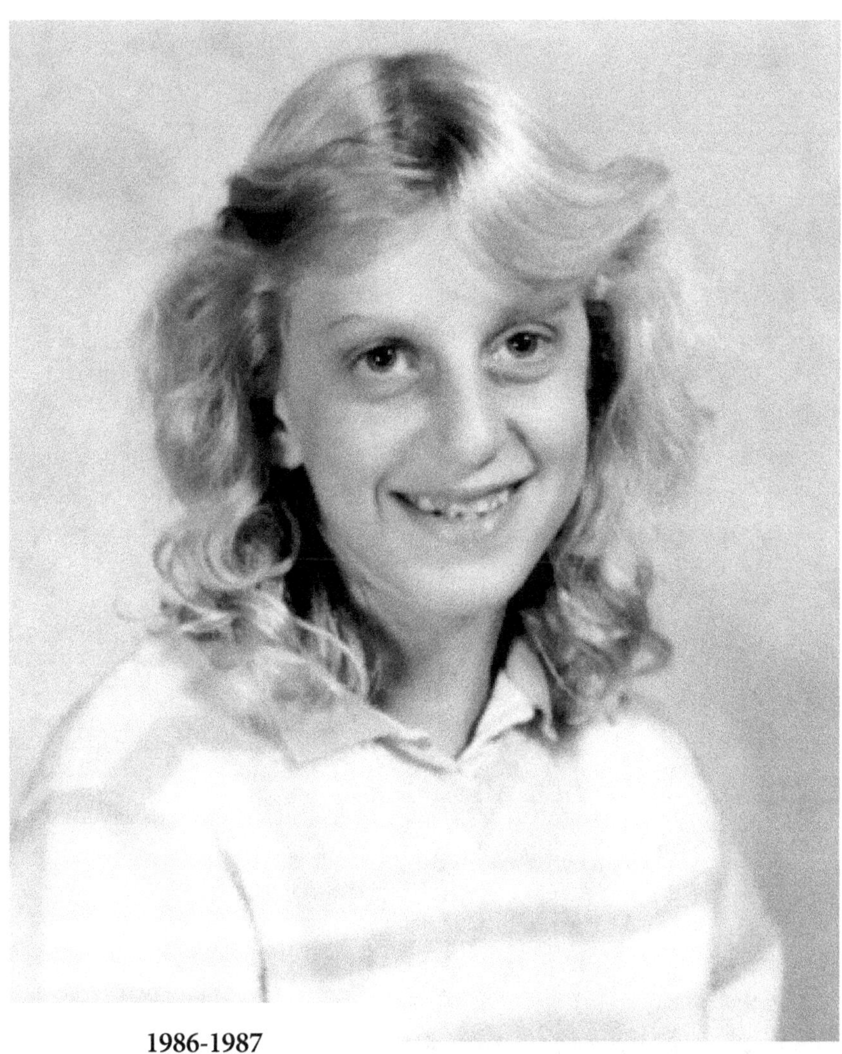

1986-1987
8th Grade
13 Years Old,

Violin orchestra, babysitting,
Traveled to Savannah, GA with
Girl Scouts to Cabbage Patch
Kids Center

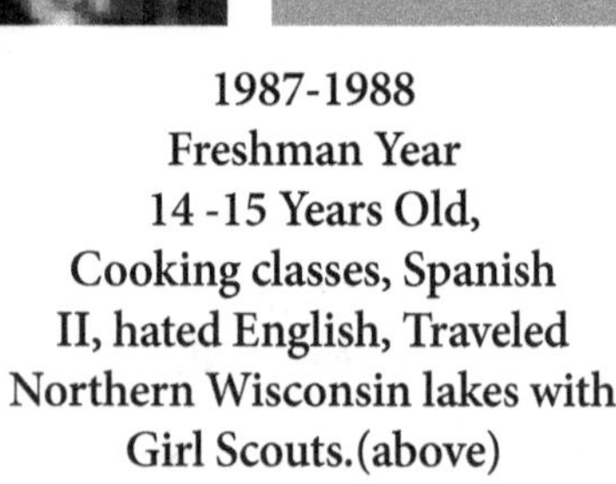

1987-1988
Freshman Year
14 -15 Years Old,
Cooking classes, Spanish
II, hated English, Traveled
Northern Wisconsin lakes with
Girl Scouts.(above)

1991
High School Senior (left)

May 1999
Traveling with friends to
Washington, DC often

2000
Visiting the waterfalls in
Northern Wisconsin (above)

2002
Graduation from Marquette
Law School (right)

2001
Right before my law school
graduation (left)

December 2002
Florida trip: Christmas right
before life started imploding.

Blood clot/ PE, divorce,
memories surface of sexual
abuse (above)

2010
Mercy, the first teen I developed a relationship with in Kenya. She is now the namesake of the home for girls in Vipingo. (left)

With a Kenyan child. (above)

2009
With a Kenyan child.(top)

With the staff at Bomani
(center)

2016
Kerry and I
(Tiwi, Kenya) (right)

Chapter 5

MY RELATIONSHIPS STOLEN

As the shame was building bigger and bigger in the pit of my stomach and shames voice was ringing louder and louder in my head, it led to strong feelings.

Disgust is not a word that I normally associate with its own category of emotion. Some of the synonyms are:

- Disapproval of who I was
- Disappointment in me and my choices
- My perception that everyone thought I was awful
- Avoidance of everyone

Many of these are words were exactly what my attackers used directly on me. You had better believe these words summed up who I thought I was as a person. **I was disgusting.**

Trying to have a healthy relationship when disgust is how you feel about yourself puts you in a bad spot and subject to a lot of trouble. That is if you are brave enough to even get close in a relationship which usually doesn't happen. No matter what someone tells you, it will never be as powerful as what you tell yourself. The people who will enter a relationship are even less healthy. They are usually abusive in many ways.

I was a ticking time bomb. The façade of perfectionism and people-pleasing led me down some dangerous roads. The lack of boundaries was a huge problem. *I'll give you everything you want. Just don't abandon me like everyone else has.* Lack of trust and putting myself into the hands of untrustworthy people was a huge problem. I couldn't trust myself. I had made such poor decisions. Even though I made horrible choices in boyfriends, I trusted them to take care of me. I had a sense of over responsibility to take care of everything and everyone around me. This led to being responsible for everything. There was nowhere that this was more destructive than in my first serious boyfriend relationship.

We left off my story of me telling my friend about the rape and her reaction not going so well for me. Fast-forward a year or so and it was finally time for a "real" relationship. I finally had the boyfriend I had always dreamed of. Well, maybe it wasn't what I dreamed of, but at least it was a boyfriend. Following are some excerpts from a diary I wrote about that time in my life–years after the events had transpired, with the names changed.

CARRIE'S DIARY

Who knew that in a little less than a year and my life would never be the same again. It all started near the end of my senior year of high school. Life started to get way off track. I started making very poor choices with no reason for them at all. My mind was cluttered.

I had an intense desire for a boyfriend all through high school. I had a few dance partners and talking friends, but not much more than that. I would fantasize about "my" boyfriend – what color of eyes, hair, etc. I would think about, "What if that pool boy was my boyfriend?" It was constantly in my thoughts at the time.

I needed someone to tell me that I was good enough and that I was lovable. The first person who showed me any attention I jumped at. Jim was it. He lived in an efficiency apartment, had no job, and had a small child. In hindsight, he was not the ideal candidate, but I was more than willing to overlook that.

This led to a complete lack of any boundaries. I would do whatever it took to get one and keep one. I did not have any other criteria for that boyfriend. Therein laid the problem.

His friend Mitch would drive us around. Mitch was a great guy. I probably liked Mitch more than I liked Jim, but I was too afraid and shy to say anything to Mitch. Mitch was a good guy and wouldn't like me anyway.

The "good guys" wouldn't want me. Even if they did at first, once they really got to know me they wouldn't. I had nothing to offer them other than what they already had, so why would they stay with me? Even when I really liked a good guy, I would totally ignore him. I wouldn't answer his calls or the door if he stopped by. I did this to protect myself and him. No one would ever want me if I told them what had happened.

I didn't want me. No good guy should have to deal with me. I knew this. I didn't know how to deal with this. My best girl friend since 3rd grade wanted no part in helping me, so why would he?

VIOLENCE AND INAPPROPRIATE RESPONSES

I felt good around him at first, I thought. Jim seemed to respect his parents. We dated for maybe two months (April and May), and in early June, I had my first experience with sex on the floor of his basement apartment. I cried and cried. It hurt and was not what I thought it would be. It produced flashbacks of early abuse.

It was a nightmare but I kept it to myself. I suppressed the thoughts and feelings and just kept moving on. I wasn't going to let myself be abandoned, rejected, and alone again. To prevent this from happening, I felt I had no choice. I had to sleep with him or he would go somewhere else. I had no trust in him or myself.

I had no boundaries at all. I did it to keep him. I didn't know the first thing about relationships or sex for that matter. I knew I wouldn't get anyone else. I was worthless and unworthy. I was desperate. I needed him to prove my worth.

I had my goal, a boyfriend, and no one was going to take that from me. It took way too long to find one and I wasn't going to let this go. It was not because of sex or lack of sex. It wasn't because my family and/or friends didn't like him. The lies and secrets, which I already was an expert in, led me further away from the few relationships I did have with friends in my life in this relationship.

LEGAL TROUBLE

One afternoon, Jim was driving through West Allis. A cop pulled him over. He got out of the car and started to run. I knew he did not have a driver's license. However, I let him drive anyway. I was again putting trust in someone who didn't deserve it. After he left, I stayed with the car. In the backseat of the car, there was a stolen stereo. I was now involved because it was in my car. I didn't know it was stolen at the time.

I acted like a moron. I tried to be an overly responsible hero to him by not giving the cops his name. I received two tickets for it— lying to a cop and receiving stolen property. The cops called my house and my brother gave the cops my mom's work number.

I was mad at my family for ruining the cover-up. This still was not even near an eye opener for me. I just wanted a boyfriend and I saw my family standing in the way of that.

In mid-June, Jim went to his brother's wedding. Drinking

and violence had been an issue for us many times by this point. He got really drunk and violent (physically and sexually). I still didn't even think about leaving. I don't even remember the details.

It was probably at this point that he started to rekindle his relationship with his previous ex-girlfriend that he had a one-year-old child with. I was completely aware of it. We went out after he was done with her. He, of course, was only seeing her to avoid child support. There were no boundaries and I couldn't handle being rejected again.

LIES & SECRETS

On my end, I started telling white lies to my family and friends, which led to bigger lies. At the end of the relationship, I was living life in secret and alone. I felt abandoned and rejected many times. I would leave the house at all hours. Because I spent all my time on this relationship that was not worth fighting for, I damaged relationships with my mom, dad, brother, friends, roommates, and others.

I didn't spend much time at school. I would come home almost every day. I brought Jim up to the dorm a few times. Once, while he was drunk, he got mad. He got out of the car and started walking all around. I was frantically looking for him all over and freaking out. How would he get home? Where would he stay? I had to find him. It was his own stupid fault but I felt completely responsible. I had no boundaries and was overly responsible for him.

My parents were starting to go through a divorce. He got me out of my house all the time and away from having to deal with my parents, brother, and any thoughts of my past. I saw him as my rescuer from that situation.

The amount of control that he had over me was ridiculous. I don't know what I thought I needed to happen to end this relationship. I think I didn't see an option of it not working after I had sex with him. We had to work it out.

A part of me was ripped off and left with Jim, because I had sex before I should have and before I was ready. It led me into a really bad place where I did anything to save the relationship. However, it was not savable or save-worthy in the first place. I was fighting for a relationship that was not even close to being worthy of fighting for. His drinking and probable drug use affected me greatly. I did anything I could to save the relationship. I felt out of control and completely responsible for him.

FINANCIAL ISSUES & OVER-RESPONSIBILITY

Lack of boundaries regarding money became a big issue in our relationship. At one point early in our relationship, he gave me a gold nugget ring that was his pride and joy. Somehow it got thrown out the window of my car, as he was driving to his mom's house. I felt extremely guilty. In my sense of over-responsibility, I thought I had to fix my huge mistake. Therefore, we made our first trip to the jewelry store and purchased a very expensive ring.

He was so happy. Since he was happy, I was happy. It brought him closer to me. We made several other stops to the jewelry store after that. In the fall, I didn't have a job because I had started college full-time. Therefore, the collection calls started. I spent a lot of my money on him. I would borrow money from my dad to spend on him. I would stress about getting approved for credit for jewelry for him. One time almost a year into it, I bought myself a ring. However, I returned it.

This financial mess kept me stuck for many, many years after that relationship ended. I would have frequent collection calls. Fox's Jewelry sued me and garnished my check. The very late payments from when I did not have a job and the settling of the accounts for a lower amount affected my credit for several years. It led me at times to steal to pay my bills. The lack of boundaries in my finances produced many problems for me.

College should have been a fresh start for me. However, I continued the relationship with Jim, which was a big mistake.

I was putting more and more money into this relationship when I said I wanted out. The intense desire to get paid back and to get my stuff back was strong. A friend simply said, "Carrie, can't you see you are pouring more and more time, money, and energy into this, and not getting anything back?"

IT GETS WORSE

In January 1992, I was scheduled for major surgery. In an effort to get relief from my migraines, the doctors had taken some scans. It was determined that I had a massive cyst in my sinus. It was so large that it was pressing on my orbital bone. They were concerned they would have to restructure my orbital bone.

Jim had no place to live, so he was living with a friend on his couch. Right before the surgery, we had sex in his friend's hallway. The next day, I went in for major surgery that took several hours. I was in the hospital for a few days.

A month later, I was getting really sick in my 8 a.m. biology class. I couldn't figure out why. At first, I thought I just had the flu. But when it went on for over a week, I went to Planned Parenthood. I took a pregnancy test and it showed some very unwanted news. I was pregnant at 19, while unemployed, in tremendous debt for jewelry, and in college. I was in a horribly controlling, violent, and abusive relationship. He was also dating his ex-girlfriend with whom he had a 2-year-old child.

I felt very alone and abandoned. I didn't know what to do. This relationship led me to lies and secrecy. Therefore, none of my family and friends knew anything about it. I had really just disappeared from life, except for school, work, and him.

I was in real trouble with nowhere to turn and nowhere to go. I felt alone, rejected, and abandoned again. I also now had a huge issue to figure out.

I didn't feel like I could talk with anyone older (I now wish I would have called Corky, a previous Girl Scout leader.) I felt so isolated in my relationship with Jim that I felt I had no one to count on. Everything was very secret. I knew I could not talk to my parents. I was afraid of my mom and my dad was not a talker.

I tried talking with two friends. They didn't have the knowledge base to make this hard decision. One shared that I should keep it and do whatever it took. The other shared that she had the same experience during her senior year of high school with a boyfriend. She had an abortion. Their opinions canceled each other's out.

Jim then called me from his "new girlfriend's" house. At some point in the conversation, she came on the phone. It turned out that she was the mother of his then almost 2-year-old child. She threatened me. If I didn't have an abortion, she would see to it that her brothers took care of the situation for me. I have no idea what that meant, but I was living in fear of the relationship and this didn't help. I was abandoned, rejected, and alone again.

I had nowhere to turn. I did not know what to do. These were some of the thoughts running through my head at the time:

• The fear was overwhelming

• I thought about how the violence and abuse of the relationship was affecting me physically, financially, and emotionally. This produced even more fear in me. What if I didn't do what he wanted me to do? What would he do to me? Would he kill me? How could I live with him in a relationship with a kid for the rest of my life?

• I could not look perfect from the outside. I had to keep up the illusion of perfection. This would RUIN that. Everyone would know. Everyone would judge me. Everyone would be disappointed in me. Everyone would hate me. Everyone would abandon me. Everyone would finally know for sure that I wasn't good enough. I wasn't worth it.

• The thought of adoption never entered my mind. I'm not sure why. I'm guessing it was because if adoption was an option, EVERYONE would know and I would not be the perfect person I needed to believe I was to get through life.

• If I wanted to continue with school, how would I take care of this baby? I could not do both—have the baby and finish school. That was not an option.

In a haze of fear and confusion, I called the Metropolitan Health Clinic. I asked them what to do logistically. They said I had to hurry and get in and told me how much an abortion cost.

It was all scheduled and then a snowstorm hit. I could not get anyone to drive me. I called everyone. No one could come and get me. I saw this as God trying to keep me from making a big mistake. However, I was determined, desperate, and afraid.

Jim's friend ended up driving to Whitewater in a bad snowstorm to pick me up. I was afraid for my life driving back to Milwaukee in the blowing and drifting snow, but we got there.

He drove me to the clinic on 26th and Wisconsin. He gave me the money, sent me in, and left me abandoned, rejected, and alone. The whole process felt like an out of body experience. I can remember lying there on the table in a dark room. I was just numb, with no feeling or thoughts and totally empty, while they scrapped my uterus. I terminated the pregnancy.

When the procedure was done and I was in the recovery room, they told me Jim was there to pick me up. My blood pressure rose and the nurse was concerned. She encouraged me to leave him. The light finally went on. I knew I had to get out of the relationship. I knew I needed to start again.

Jim then drove me home to New Berlin and left me there in the house all abandoned, rejected, and alone.

As far as I know, the only ones who knew about it were my two friends, my boyfriend, and his two friends. I felt like the baby was a boy. His name would have been Brandon. His due date would have been October, 1992.

That was the end of what felt like eternity, but was not even a year. I had finally broken free from that destructive relationship. I don't think he kept up on the relationship either, but I don't remember clearly. I hope others won't have to go to that extreme to break off a bad relationship.

The relationship with Jim caused me to be the worst I ever was, both emotionally and spiritually. I was desperate and alone, with nothing to fill it with except for him. Sex is a sacred and special thing. For me, to give that away outside of marriage, especially for a girl, is too difficult emotionally. Because my feelings and emotions were so depressed, shut down, I didn't have much to offer in a relationship other than sex. My thought was this is how all men were. They want/need sex. Because of this untrue belief, I had offered sex which was too early for me emotionally. Now I realize any relationship prior to marriage is too early. However, that is a story for another book.

I had sex within one-and-a-half-months of meeting my first "boyfriend." It was an equally horrible experience on the floor of his basement apartment. It was not good at all. It hurt. In fact, it was unbearable. It was almost as horrible as the original trauma.

The result kept me in this relationship, even after I knew it should have been over with. It was an abusive relationship physically, emotionally and even sexually. It led to unprotected sex and an abortion. I thank God to this day that it did not lead to any sexually transmitted diseases, which could have led to death or being unable to have kids. I wish I had acknowledged my need for help sooner. I wish I had made different decisions. This relationship and the choices I made in it, led to me dropping out of college and heading down a different path.

Having no boundaries, putting trust in shady people and being overly responsible for someone else, led me down a road full of huge problems.

I was codependent. My being OK was completely dependent on him being OK. When you turn your own personal power completely over to someone else to control, you are in for the ride of your lifetime. I don't mean it in a good way.

At the time, he was probably my savior from my home life, which I didn't feel I fit into. I felt abandoned, rejected and alone in my home. It was the result of the early abuse. However, it was made even worse by the divorce and I didn't even know it. He was my connection and distraction. I was desperate for worthiness and having him made me feel worthy. Nothing else could.

I turned to alcohol, friends, and fun to numb the pain. I decided I would drop out of regular college. I decided to learn bartending and to make a living that way. Drinking was my top priority. All of these experiences left me saying, "How did I get here? How could I do these things?" At this point, I just wanted to numb the pain. I didn't even have the energy to whisper, **"I Just Want My Life Back!"**

I knew my life was over. The silence continued and so did the pain for me and those around me. The stakes were about to become higher very quickly. There was so much more trouble before it got better.

Chapter 6

BAD CHOICES, SITUATIONS, AND CONSEQUENCES

I was living life numbing the feelings and running away from my problems. I was drinking every night. I would get up, go to work at sometimes two or three jobs, go to school, and then hit the bars with friends until 2 or 3 a.m. every night. I did this without fail. I was running and running. I was also numb - so numb. I would fix everyone else's problems and pretend I didn't have any of my own.

At some point, the financial aspect of working at a day care with a college degree kicked in. If I had to pay for college, working at a day care center with an early childhood education degree was not going to be very profitable. Therefore, I changed to child psychology. I thought I could do more to protect kids through that service and make more money doing it.

I was unaware at the time to become a psychologist you had to go to graduate school. I also really had no idea what a child psychologist did every day. I got a job in a psychologist's office. I thought, "Awesome, I will be living my dream!"

I hated every moment of working at the psychologist's office. It felt like parents who were unable to control their kids brought them to the psychologist in order to fix them. (That is not accurate, and now, having had teenagers, I totally get it.) However, I knew being a psychologist was not for me. In fact, it was the first job I was ever fired from.

I really enjoyed my time at the law office as far as the work was concerned. I loved the rigid, well-defined rules. I excelled and really enjoyed it. I found another job at a different law office and worked there all through the rest of my 11 total years of schooling.

On the other hand, I had no idea what I was going to do after graduating from undergraduate school. I had determined I didn't want to be a psychologist, but I didn't know what to do.

I went into the career counseling office at my school. They suggested I apply to law school. That was never a thought. I told them there was no way with my grades I would get into law school. As I mentioned, my grades were good, but because of my 5-credit of D's in math, my grade point was a 2.73.

However, the thought of having that much knowledge, power, and control over people appealed greatly to me. No one could keep me in a relationship. No one would be smarter than me in most rooms, if I could pull this one off. Everyone would love me. Everyone would want to be around me. I would have a lot to offer everyone around me.

I had no confidence that I would be accepted, but did apply to law school. After a short stint on the wait list, I was accepted into the Marquette Law School in the fall of 1997!

I was on my way to having the only thing I ever wanted in this world. Control over my life! Finally.

BAD CHOICES & SITUATIONS

Because I was running and trying to numb the pain and because of the fear of abandonment and rejection, the relationships I chose were toxic situations where I could help someone. If I was there to help to make them better, they would not reject me. Since they were getting something from me, they would stay. It also gave me a purpose. Just being me wasn't enough. There had to be more. I deserved the bad guys. I would stay in inappropriate relationships, because that's what I deserved. Some of them were abusive physically, sexually, and emotionally.

Following are some excerpts from a dairy I wrote years after the events occurred.

CARRIE'S DIARY
RELATIONSHIP STORIES

After the mess I had made with Jim, my plan was to drink, hang with friends, and have fun forever. I would drink nightly to the point of puking.

My plan was to drop out of college and go to bartending school. This was before I had my first law office job. I was working a part-time catering job. I was not doing much other than drinking. I was numbing the pain and doing my best to run from everything.

I researched a few places to attend bartending school. However, it was more expensive than I had anticipated, so I did not follow up on it.

Somehow in August, I ended up in a place I didn't expect. I actually started a relationship with a "good guy." We started dating and we had a really good relationship. With that stability in my life, I rushed to register and get together financial aid for my second year at Whitewater at his prompting. He made me feel there might be something really small inside of me that might be worthy.

After about five or six months, the emotional emptiness and extreme fear still inside of me was taking its toll on the relationship. He broke up with me in early February of the following year. It was the best relationship I had ever had. It taught me a few things. I am grateful to him for pulling my head out of the sand and getting me back on track with what was really important: school—not drinking constantly.

After that relationship, I had dates with a few other people over the next year. I spent a lot of time with a group of guys. There was one guy I liked, but he was as emotionally stuck as I was, if not worse. If we all have one relationship that we wonder what could have been, he would have been one of those for me. Both his and my unexpressed silence left many things unspoken.

NEXT RELATIONSHIP

Instead, I moved on to the next person that showed any interest. Again, jumping into a relationship with the first breathing body with no criteria or boundaries. I used this relationship to run from what could have been a good relationship, out of fear and hurting from the emotions of the abortion and the early childhood trauma.

There was obviously a drinking problem. He was in a bar fight on the first night we met up and kissed. Felony criminal charges were filed. It was a great start to a beautiful relationship!

Within one month of being together, we had a physical relationship, which was the best part of our relationship.

We had some physical altercations early in relationship but then that disappeared. Because of drinking and violence, we broke up numerous times. However, we ended up back together.

IGNORED EMOTIONS: FINDING OUTWARD EXPRESSIONS

I decided that after about a year of this rocky relationship, I NEEDED a baby. To keep running, I needed to add another thing to the circus. It would replace what I lost.

It was time. My dream was always to have a baby. A lot of

girls dream of their wedding. I dreamed of my nursery. It was time to get pregnant.

In March, 1995, I was purposeful about getting pregnant and it worked. I was very excited.

I broke up with him in August 1995, because he kept going out to the bar. At some point, he called me and we got back together.

FINALLY, A MOM

On December 3, 1995, after being almost 2 weeks late, I was laying on the couch on a Sunday and my water broke. Colton came into the world, after two hours of pushing by being sucked out of me at about 10:45 am on December 4, 1995. He was 9 pounds, 14.5 ounces. He was a big boy. I had gained a lot of weight with him. I was still going to school at Whitewater. I had finals shortly after I had Colton. I was blessed with an amazing family and friends surrounding me and helping me with him.

I loved being a mom. He was a good baby. It was easy having one. There were no distractions.

I was applying for law school, finishing undergraduate school, and working a few jobs.

However, to keep running, I needed something else to distract me. I needed to move on to something.

MARRIAGE?

At some point in the spring/early summer, we got engaged at my prompting. I spent the summer planning the wedding—dresses, shoes, reception hall, flowers, etc.

I was having a hard time paying the bills. The collection calls started again. My money was going towards the wedding instead of credit card payments.

By September 1996, it was obvious I should not be getting married. Various friends that did not know each other shared their concerns I shouldn't be getting married. They all practically begged me not to go through with it. I knew it was a bad idea because of the drinking and so many other warning signs.

However, I needed to look perfect. I couldn't go back now. I was too embarrassed to turn back time and went forward anyway. There was not even a thought of not going through with it, although I knew deep down that we shouldn't be getting married.

We got married at Hales Corners Lutheran Church. The wedding was very nice.

The next weekend we went to Florida for our honeymoon. It was a disaster. First, he was nowhere to be found when we were to be driving to the airport to leave early on Saturday morning. He had gone out drinking the night before. He threw up the whole way there on the plane. Once we got there, we got in a fight at some point and he threw his wedding ring into the crab grass at the timeshare condo we were staying in. Nice start to the marriage.

GOD'S PAY BACK

I was pregnant at the wedding, although no one knew. It was weird because my dress had to be taken in. I was due in June. On New Year's Eve 1996-1997, I went for an ultrasound. They could not find the heartbeat. They sent me to the doctor's office without telling me what was going on.

I had to walk around with a dead baby in me for a week or more, until they scheduled the delivery. I had to fully deliver the baby. I was 6-months pregnant. I went through a full labor. It was horrible and my mom wasn't there. It was only my husband because I didn't think it would be such a big deal. We found out afterwards that it was a girl, which is what I wanted. Brianna. January,1997.

He told me the cord was too long and wrapped around the neck of the baby. I had done a handstand a few months earlier and thought it might have been because of that. I felt that God was getting back at me for having an abortion.

I didn't talk to anyone about the abortion. It was another thing I was running from. I was pretending that it wasn't affecting me. If someone admitted their abortion to me, then I would share. However, I would never be the first to share.

One of the two friends who I had shared with when I was trying to make the decision, felt it okay to share for me. She, a person who had two abortions herself, felt it was okay for her to share my details with people behind my back. When I heard about it, the two times she shared about it, I started freaking out. I needed to be perfect and look perfect. She was ruining that.

It was a very stressful time.

WIFE AND MARRIAGE

I moved back in with Dad because I had gotten into law school. I didn't want the great financial stress of supporting everything by myself with my husband's employment instability. I was working two jobs and had a child.

However, I also brought my own problems and struggles to the marriage. They were a lot more hidden for sure, but placed just as much stress on the situation. Anxiety and fear often overwhelmed me. I was trying to keep everything and everyone "safe" all the time. I didn't even know what that meant. I was trying desperately to control things to do this.

There was general sadness. I didn't even know why I was sad. I was sad that I was not being the mom I wanted or hoped I would be. I was also sad that the marriage wasn't what I hoped it would be. I was distant and fearful. I was always moving—shopping, projects, work, school, something.

I was pissed off I had to deal with behaviors that were unacceptable, which led to a lack of forgiveness, bitterness, and anger.

Underlying everything was a fear of being abandoned, rejected, and alone again.

MOM AGAIN

I found out I was pregnant with Brooklyn in October 1997 and had been pregnant since August. I had just started law school. It was really hard to think when pregnant. On May 4, 1998, I went into labor during a final exam in Torts class. I didn't do very well on the test.

In August 1998, Brooklyn was baptized. Brooklyn's dad almost didn't show up. He was hung over. After Brooklyn was born, the drinking got worse. He would not come home at night. He was probably doing drugs too. When he did come home, it was worse. I would yell and my stomach was in knots. It was not good. I hated it, but I didn't know what to do. I would get in fits of rage about his drinking. There was yelling and screaming. I was getting frustrated dealing with his drinking and the interaction between the kids, which made it hard to focus. There was also school and work.

My lack of patience was a recurring problem and kept me from being the mom I wanted to be. I had so much to keep control over, including my life and safety. I also had my secrets to keep. I had to control my husband's drinking and anything else he might have been doing. I also had to keep all the money coming in to pay all the bills for me and the kids. I had to keep the kids safe and do everything that needed to be done for them. I had to do everything that was expected of me for law school and both of my jobs. Frustration was a common occurrence. Rushing and yelling was a regular occurrence.

The distance I had kept in relationships in order to keep me safe was probably even there in my relationship with my kids. Fear and shame kept me from being closer than I would have liked to be with my kids when they were older. We were always on the go, at someone's house, shopping, or doing something.

MORE TRAUMA AND DRAMA

In December 2000, my husband was driving drunk and hit a car with two girls in it. He had been at a work Christmas party. He smashed into the car so hard that his head went through the window on the other side of the truck. He was inches away from hitting the frame of the truck, which would have probably killed him.

I was home studying and dealing with our kids—who were then 3- and 5-years-old. I got a call from Froedert Hospital telling me he was in an accident and that I needed to come to the hospital. It was three days before Christmas. Within a few days, he was home and "fine." This car accident slowed his drinking down some, but not for good.

After the accident, because he had no car insurance, and because he had the possibility of a drunk-driving incident, we had to use money to pay for a lawyer. The lawyer actually was able to get the District Attorney to not file charges against him. The police officer did not take the girl's blood alcohol level, even though she admitted to drinking that night, I saved him.

He was out of criminal trouble. I ended up with trouble because the car was titled in my name. He was driving and did not have insurance. We needed the lawyer to reinstate my driver's license and registration. I was in drama because of him.

TRYING MY BEST TO KEEP IT TOGETHER— NOT THE MOM I HAD ENVISIONED I WOULD BE

Colton started real school in September 2001. I cried, since my baby was going to a big, big school and he was so little. It was during this time-period when Colton missed the bus. I lost it and was yelling and yelling at him. I was out of control.

I was afraid of being abandoned, rejected, and being alone with kids. It kept me from being the parent that I wanted to be.

HELP IN MY SPIRITUAL JOURNEY

In August, 2001, my neighbor came over and told me about Alanon, an organization for the families of drinkers or drug addicts. He had overheard my husband at a neighborhood party talk about his drinking and thought I might benefit.

This was a major life-changing moment, although I did not know it at the time. It was a huge step in my spirituality. It brought me a little back on track in my head. Alanon explained how my reaction was my problem and his drinking was his problem. That was helpful. I started kind of slow. Soon, I was attending meetings a few times a week. I loved the meetings and would go to open AA meetings sometimes in order to gain their perspective, which helped. After awhile I got a sponsor. It took a few years. I chose an older woman who attended both of my main meetings. Her name was Barb. She was awesome. She had a lot of years under her belt. She did a great job working with me through the steps. She was the first person I had ever told about the abortion. It was a great introduction to spirituality.

In May, 2002, I went through the ceremony for law school graduation. I was really sick with strep throat. I always seemed to get sick around finals time.

I finally slowed down at this time to celebrate for a day. It lasted for one minute.

After graduating from law school, I quit my job to look for full-time work. Within 2 months I had a position at a very prestigious law firm in the Milwaukee area!

A FEW LESSONS LEARNED

I was always running from my problems. I didn't want to face all the problems of my history, some of which I didn't even know about yet. I was turning to people and activities (law school) as distractions.

Perfection led me down destructive paths. I wanted everyone to think I was perfect. If it didn't look like perfection, I wouldn't even consider it. I would hold up the appearance and deal with whatever I had to deal with, for the behind-the-scenes consequences to keep the outward appearance. I would lie, cheat, steal, and stay in a horrible marriage.

By the age of 22, I had kids and was married. I did what I had to do to get by. On the outside, everything looked perfect. I continued on to law school after college, worked two jobs, supported my kids by myself, and paid all the bills. I then graduated and was a practicing lawyer for six years. But on the inside, my husband drank too much. He didn't come home at times and was very difficult to live with.

I'm sure I was no walk in the park, either. I was extremely controlling of everything in my environment and now I know it was due to the traumatic experiences. I need you all to know I was miserable. I had a good front so no one would know. My front was so good I didn't even think I needed any help. I didn't know any other way of life. This was normal. I did not know there was anything else. The saddest part was I thought everyone felt and lived like this. However, inside I was screaming, "I Just Want My Life Back!"

Soon I just might have that long-lost wish, but what it would take to get it was almost more than I could pay.

Chapter 7

UNTIL IT CAME FLOODING BACK ...

From the outside looking in, things looked really good. I had graduated from undergraduate school with a degree in psychology. I went on to apply, get accepted, and finish law school on the Dean's List. I was married with a healthy boy and girl. From the outside looking in, things looked good. I had just turned 30. I was not even a full year into my practice of law, working at a great firm. I loved my work and worked for great people at a top law firm in the city, in my area of law. Through perfectionism, achievements, and control, life looked great on the outside.

Inside, alcohol and drugs were tearing my family and perfect life apart. My husband was staying out all night long and not coming home. His going out to the bar and coming home drunk in the middle of night resulted in my yelling and screaming. There was also a drunk-driving accident. My unhealed past was making things one-hundred times worse.

My lack of patience and need for control kept me from being anywhere near the parent that I wanted to be. There was more yelling than talking. I was not living up to my expectations of myself as a mom in almost every way. I was running from my emotions by always being on the move at someone's house or shopping. Things then came crashing down really quickly.

FEBRUARY 2003—DEATH IS NEAR

In January, I had gone for my annual check-up. I had gained some weight while being on the DEPO shot for birth control. My best friend was getting married in September and I was in the wedding and I wanted to lose weight I had gained on this birth control. So, I talked to the doctor and started using the patch for birth control.

Not long after that, I began to get side aches and stomach pains. It didn't seem too major. It only hurt when I laughed too hard or did certain things. One morning, I got up early to make my way to the gym at the office. I did my normal workout. Everything went well and I was up in my office to begin my day.

In the middle of the morning, I had this tremendous pain in my calf. It came out of nowhere. I thought that maybe I pulled a muscle working out and didn't think much of it. I elevated my leg under my desk, but it kept getting worse and worse really fast. By mid-afternoon, I was heading to a doctor. My doctor couldn't fit me in, so I went to urgent care near my house.

I explained my calf started hurting really bad in the morning and had gotten worse and worse. It seemed to come out of nowhere. I had worked out but I didn't feel anything during the work out. As they asked what prescriptions I was on, I shared I had switched birth control recently. The nurse made careful notes and asked many questions about this.

The doctor came in and didn't say much. He prescribed a muscle relaxer for me and sent me home. I went home, went upstairs to bed to elevate my leg and took the muscle relaxer. The next morning, I woke up and couldn't walk on that leg. I had to crawl down the stairs. Sometime in the early morning, I hopped to the downstairs bathroom and saw that my thigh was swollen and gray in color. I called the doctor immediately and went back in. By this point, I couldn't walk. I arrived on crutches. He looked, sent me for an X-ray, and said he didn't see anything. He gave me some pain pills and sent me home again.

I slept in the recliner because I could not walk up the stairs. At about 3 a.m., I couldn't stand the pain anymore. My leg felt hot, my foot was freezing cold, and I started to cough. I woke up my husband and told him to drive me to the hospital. As I arrived at the hospital, the nurse seemed very concerned about the coughing. They put me in a room. The place was a zoo. After a few hours, they had a technician do a Doppler scan of my leg. The technician thought he wasn't getting a reading, so they sent me for a scan on a bigger machine.

I remember sitting in the hallway outside that scan room afterwards. The hallway was empty. Lying on the gurney, I felt close to death. I also felt abandoned and alone. It was, as though, my body was rejecting me.

I had no diagnosis at that point, but I felt death near me. I was alone in the hallway for a long time. It was like an out-of-body experience. I was looking down on myself from the ceiling. I was lying there and felt cold, alone, and afraid again. I had nowhere to go, no one to turn to, and no one to trust. That is a feeling I will never forget. I've had a lot of trauma in my life but this moment was different. It was evil and it was like death was hovering over me.

ANXIETY STARTS OVERTAKING ME

After that scan, they sent me up to a hospital room. At some point, a doctor came in and told me I had a Deep Vein Thrombosis (DVT) and Pulmonary Embolism (PE.) I had no idea what that meant, although he was very clear it was not good. He asked if I changed my birth control method recently and I said yes. I had the patch and showed it to him. He ripped it off very quickly. He indicated DVT/PE's many times are fatal.

They were pumping me full of blood thinners in the hope of remedying the situation. I felt that was very odd. Why wouldn't they take me in for surgery to remove it?

The plan was to stay in the bed for 24 hours. That would include having to use a bedpan for the bathroom. That made no sense to me. It started to increase my anxiety to high levels.

As the hours passed, I came to realize more about the blood clot in my leg (DVT) and my lungs (PE) which almost killed me. During the first evening, a visiting extended family member came to see me at the hospital. She felt it was necessary to share that her friend had died of the same thing the week before.

As I lay in the hospital room day after day, I kept asking when I could go home. It seemed every day they indicated possible discharge later today or tomorrow, but each day, it was followed by the same statement, not today. Staying in the hospital was making my anxiety worse. I was scared and alone most of the time. I had no control over anything. I also had way too much time to think. Each day got worse and worse.

Not only was it a breeding ground for negative thoughts and way too much time to think about them, they were constantly taking blood from me to check my blood clotting levels. The IV gave me black and blue arms from my wrists to my shoulders. At some point early on, I was getting poked every hour to check my blood clotting levels. It was reduced later in the week, but the IV was constant and had to be changed multiple times. It was miserable. I never liked needles and now I am extremely fearful of them.

On about the 3rd or 4th day in the hospital, a reporter who was on assignment with the military got out of an army tank and stumbled to his death. It was all over the TV set in front of me in the hospital. He died of the same thing I was sitting in the hospital with, a DVT/PE. My anxiety was through the roof.

I had lost all faith in the medical system and was terrified of every doctor. The doctor at the urgent care had misdiagnosed me big time. That was obvious from my discussions with the doctors. With the change of birth control and the calf pain, it was a sure sign of a blood clot. The doctor should have known, It is a classic sign. That is why the nurse was so concerned in the pre-interview. I was afraid to trust this new doctor in the hospital who I did not know at all.

I was grateful for my OB/GYN who spent one hour or more talking with me on the phone while I was in the hospital, explaining what was going on. He indicated the stomach pains from earlier in the month were part of this whole thing. I begged for him to be my doctor but he did not have privileges there. I needed a different type of doctor, a vascular specialist.

At some point, while I was in the hospital, the anxiety I had kept under "control" all these years started showing through in major ways. I had severe heart pain. The fear, sadness, and lack of trust in people and even myself, was SO overwhelming that my body could not keep it in line anymore.

It was to the point that the hospital had to do a full heart scan work-up on me. They found nothing. I was very fearful the doctors did not know what they were doing. I had a doctor with a foreign accent I could not understand. In my distress, I asked her to leave. I asked for a new doctor for these tests. Although I don't recall the specifics of the conversation, I don't believe it was done in a very nice way.

I was in the hospital for eight days. On the eighth day, I may have left without full consent of the doctor, but I couldn't do it anymore. It was a prison I was unable to get out. I had no control over anything–my body, my situation, and my "perfect" world was starting to unravel before my eyes. I had to get out. Fear and anxiety were waging war in my mind. My own body had now turned against me. Now, I could trust literally no one. I couldn't even trust myself. I was out of my rational mind.

I couldn't walk for months and things were very difficult at home. I couldn't go to the kitchen to get something to eat or drink. I couldn't go back to work. I needed to keep my leg elevated at all times in the beginning. I couldn't help my kids, who were seven and four at the time. I couldn't function myself. But wait…it gets worse.

INFIDELITY/DIVORCE

One week after I came home from the hospital, my husband announced he was leaving me. After everything I had done for him and put up with, all his drinking, drunk-driving, and other issues, HE was leaving ME. At the time, he left out the fact he was leaving me for a former best friend of mine and was moving out to move in with her.

My "perfect" world was crumbling all around me. So there I was at home, having almost died a week before, unable to walk without crutches, with a seven- and a four-year-old child to take care of… and he was leaving. I was abandoned, rejected and alone yet again. In my deepest time of need...

ANXIOUS THOUGHTS OUT OF CONTROL

My family life was all a side issue though. I could not stop thinking the blood clot was still going to kill me. The fear of my own body letting me down was overwhelming. I was unable to wrap my head around it. I had always been an anxious person but I could usually function through the anxiety. I could even use it to make me or a situation better. No matter what I did, I could not get the thought out of my mind, "You should be dead." Over the past 28 years, those same words had been repeated over and over again in my head.

Overwhelmed, I ended up back in the hospital one week later because of fear the clot was returning. I felt my doctors were not explaining it to me like it really was. I had no trust in them at all. I needed to have control. They were giving me no way to do that. I could not stand the fact my body was rejecting me and there was nothing I could do about it. "You should be dead" rang in my head.

No matter what I tried, I could not get the thoughts out of my head or under control. I didn't know what to do. It was just like when the thoughts came flooding back of the childhood trauma. However, the difference in my mind by this point was the blood clot was real. The trauma stuff was all my fault. There was nothing I could do to control this health issue. That other stuff, if it wasn't for my stupidity, never would have happened.

After a week, I finally broke down enough to admit I needed someone to help me. I had the constant thoughts of, "You are going to die from this blood clot to your lungs and there is nothing you can do about it. You should be dead."

I was left alone with two young children. I was unable to even care for myself, let alone them. I couldn't keep it together anymore. I couldn't keep up the façade. It forced me to break the perfectionism barrier and reach out for help.

I called a psychologist. I got an appointment for a few days later. I went into the office and there was paperwork to fill out. There were many questions on the form. I filled out all of them, except for the one that asked, "Have you ever been sexually abused or raped?"

What did that matter? I was here because I almost died, my husband had left me with two little kids, and I was unable to walk. I had not had any thoughts or issues about sexual abuse or rape for many years. I simply chose to forget about it and not talk about it anymore. My life was moving along just fine. Therefore, I did not check the box.

FINALLY REACHING OUT AGAIN

We started the therapy. She listened to the drama about the blood clot and all of the consuming thoughts. She listened to me talk about the husband, and the new revelations that would occur every week on where he was living, who he was living with, all the drama that goes with the first few weeks of living apart and starting the decision-planning for a possible divorce. She was patient, kind, and caring. She also went through the form and asked me about the only question I left blank.

There I was, 30-years-old, 29 years after my first sexual abuse incident and 20 years after my second round of abuse and rape. I was in the office of a psychologist, not for the childhood trauma, but for totally different reasons. I finally admitted to another human being, out loud, that I had been sexually abused.

I refused to use the word, rape, at all. I was very clear with her I was not here for that. I was fine with that. It was not affecting my life at all. My husband and his cheating with my ex-best-friend and my medical issues were the problem. There were no issues affecting me because of the sexual abuse. I didn't even think about it anymore. It was not a big deal.

My current problems are the concern and not that stuff from 29 years ago.

Although, in the moment, I didn't feel like it had any bearing and was not a big deal at all, looking back, it was the moment. That early April afternoon in her office was when my life started going in another direction. I was finally truly past the facade of perfection and control. I was no longer trusting myself. I had given a tiny sliver of trust to another person.

IT GETS WORSE BEFORE IT GETS BETTER

The funny thing is, I say it started going in another direction. It sounds good and optimistic. It really was a living hell. That moment started the journey to discovering who I really was. Uncovering what was all done to me, what I had all lost, and what I had all done behind the façade of perfection.

The next several months of my life were agonizing. I didn't think I would be able to get through it. The vivid memories came back. It was as if they were happening in that moment all over again. I didn't have anyone there with me, other than the paid psychologist to deal with it, and a good friend that couldn't necessarily relate, though was of great support.

I worked with the psychologist. She assigned me homework through books like *The Courage to Heal* and others. In addition to the individual counseling sessions, she had me join a group counseling session that she led for woman addressing sexual abuse issues.

All of the people in the group I was in at the time did not have jobs. They had lives still consumed by the trauma. Most of them were significantly older than I was. That was scary. I had a moment with her where I screamed, "I cannot be HERE for the next 10 years!" There has to be some sunset on this trauma. My life cannot be consumed by this past forever.

This work showed me how much I was being affected by the after-effects of sexual trauma. ALL of my life had not been my own. My entire life had been governed by my reactions to the sexual abuse and trauma I had suffered. I had never had a chance to even start a life of my own.

She encouraged me to do an emotional healing weekend called *Taking It Lightly*. The weekend dealt with owning my emotions and then bringing forgiveness in. During the emotional healing workshop, we did various things. There were some physical activities, some journaling, and some lecturing on emotions and what they were.

We talked about living life on certain planes or playing fields. If we live life on the plane of "fear," our life will be like a roller-coaster and out of control. It will go forward and backwards, this way and that, and spinning in circles. If we choose to live our life on the plane of "love", life is a lot more consistent. It will be generally pointing upward to the next level. Even when there are bumps in the road, they don't throw us into circles. They help move us to the next level in the plane of life.

We also learned about how important gratitude is in staying on the "love" plane. When we are grateful for what we have in life, we stay on the "love" plane. When we are complaining, it is because we have jumped tracks and are now on the fear plane.

One of the things with the fear plane is we always take things personally. There was an acronym they asked us to remember, QTIP (Quit Taking It Personally). When people say things or do things, it is rarely about you. It is usually about them and where they are at in their life at that second. Don't take it home and stew about it for days or weeks. Don't think they hate you. Don't do anything at first. If it still bothers you in a week or so, ask the person directly what they meant by their comment. Quit Taking It Personally. On the love plane, you give people the benefit of a doubt and realize most comments and statements have nothing to do with you.

There were times of loud music and dancing and just fun. Like I explained earlier – fun was scary for me. "Fun" times are the times when these things happened to me. As a result, fun was something I had avoided for 30+ years. It was fun to have a little fun!

At some point, I had to physically and emotionally take my life back. As it turns out, my blood clot was the same medical issue that killed my first assailant. That was deeply disturbing to me. I felt like he was still controlling me and completely affecting my life from the grave. He had been dead for over 26 years by that point. However, my body was infected by the same disorder he died of. It was as if he was coming back from the dead and consuming me again.

Talk about taking my life back. As part of the exercises, it was not easy to physically fight against others (using a towel) to take back my life. It was intimidating. I gave up strength and hope many times. However, in the end, I was able to persevere. It was a very freeing moment. I don't know where the strength came from, but I did it. That very minute, my life changed 180 degrees for the better.

Other exercises helped confirm and expand those changes. I wrote a forgiveness letter to myself and the people who had done this to me. After writing the letter, I felt true freedom. That was the remaining 180 degree turn to make it come full-circle.

I cried and cried and cried.

I didn't have to keep it in any longer. It didn't have to be a secret. I didn't have to live in the shadow of it. I didn't have to hide from the people in my group and from my emotions. I could now make my own choices based on what I wanted, not being controlled by previous experiences.

It was the first time I felt unconditional love in my entire life. I remember spending Sunday sobbing. I couldn't stop. In some ways, they were good cries. In fact, they were mostly good cries. I had never felt what it felt like to be loved—ever. Fear was always first. There, in that room, even in all my emotional mess, these people showed me love and acceptance I had never experienced before.

Here was my biggest step of trust in my entire life and it went amazingly well. The people and volunteer staff were supportive and willing to accept and help me, no matter what condition I was in. At one point, we did a circle where we passed around a purple, stuffed heart. It showed we all come from the same heart originally and we shared the same heart of love together now.

From this workshop, I also learned a lot about my thoughts. They were the thoughts I used to talk to myself in my own head. Prior to the class, it was things like, "You're not good enough," "You're going to die," "Work harder and longer," and "People don't really like you." In the class, we had a bunch of affirmations we used there and at home. The biggest one for me was, "I love and accept myself exactly the way I am." This helped me to start remembering these changes in day-to-day life. There were many others, but to experience others loving and accepting me helped me to do that same thing. Repeating these words every morning helped me to remember it more and more.

My work with the psychologist and my experience at the emotional-healing workshop changed my life. I would never be the same again. I finally realized and admitted how much these traumas had affected me. By doing that, I had started getting my own life back.

My physical appearance even changed. Many people who knew me well commented I looked different. I had moved from living in-fear to living in-love and that produced a physical change in my body! I cannot begin to tell you how amazing this group was. My life was back. I could feel and be free. I took several more classes from the center. I learned more about emotions and the many effects they have on my life.

A NEW THING TO CONTROL AND BE ANXIOUS ABOUT

This new journey was amazing. Life had definitely changed. I felt freer than ever. I felt good. There was happiness and a lot of love. It felt safe. I felt a spiritual connection. I finally did not feel alone. I felt there were people I could trust.

My life was finally being defined by what I was running TO instead of what I was running FROM. That felt good.

My secrets were revealed to a group of people who were supportive of me. They even loved me despite my secrets and maybe even because of them. I have since come to realize what a HUGE burden secrets and secrecy place on our lives. I guess I have actually learned what a relief it is to share them with the RIGHT people. It is important to have safe, trustworthy people in a position to help and care for you. As a result, the untrustworthy lose their power to control you.

However, these good feelings were dependent on me. I needed to do a lot of work to maintain these feelings. I had to read the right book, watch the right show, and be in the right place, at the right time. I had to read every book and watch every show to make sure I didn't miss anything. I had to be at every class. I still had to control everything.

I felt 10,000 times better, but I was still stressed. I was now stressed about making sure I stayed on the right track. There was still so much fear. It was just different fear. There was fear of missing something and the fear of keeping the balls in the air all by myself. It was all on my shoulders. I didn't know if I had what it took to keep it up. I wondered if there was **something more to getting my life back.**

Chapter 8

LIVING A FREE LIFE

A STEP FURTHER

After counseling and the emotional healing workshop, life was good. It was 10,000 times better than before. Life was at a whole new level. Finally, at 30-years-old, I was living "my" life for the first time. It was not controlled by trauma and fear. I never knew how much it was controlling me until afterwards. For the first time, I often felt happy and safe in my life. It was amazing!

But there was still stress and anxiety. I switched from being anxious about general safety and living in fear constantly to anxiety over managing this new level of life. I had to get to ALL of the classes, read all the books, and see all the right shows. I didn't know what the "right" ones were, so I had to go to all of them. It kept me searching, striving, and hoping I was doing it all right.

SPIRITUAL HEALING

As I shared, I was not a church-goer unless forced to go by my mom. At one point in my life, one of the girls I had met at the emotional healing workshop weekend was staying at my house for the weekend. She really wanted to go to this church about 15 minutes from my house. I told her, "You can take my car, you can do whatever you would like, but I don't do church."

Well, she would not take "no" for an answer. I finally just gave up and said to myself that it was only going to be for an hour, just get it over with, and so we went. When I got there, we were late and the service had already started. There was rock music playing from the stage – I felt like I was at a concert. The music was amazing; nothing like the boring and repetitious church I had grown up in. The message was great. It was about my life; not just repeating the same prayers and words over and over like they did at the church I was at when I was a kid. They even shared from the stage their struggles with life. They made it very relatable.

It wasn't how much God hated me but that he loved me. I wanted a relationship where He would help me through life, not judge me from a distance and take pleasure in sending me to hell. There was also a noticeable absence of those annoying "churchie" people. You know the ones. The ones that say, "Come to my church. It is so awesome. You will love it." However, behind your back, they are saying bad things about you.

After a few months at the church, I was still really enjoying it. I thought for sure within a month or two, they would say something or do something to piss me off and I would be gone just like my other experiences. Then one Friday in April, I got the call. It was the call that would bring me to my knees again in despair. It was almost as low as those moments during the abuse.

It was about 10:30 p.m. on a Friday night in April. My kids were away for the weekend camping with my mom. My ex-husband's sister called to tell me that my ex-husband had died. "It was a heroin overdose," she said. I sat there for several minutes staring at the phone in disbelief. What? A 36-year-old person does not die. A person with two kids under 10 doesn't die. My parents are still alive now. I don't know how to tell my kids. How do they live without a parent? The questions kept spinning in my mind.

My head was spinning and life was feeling really out of control. They were feelings that I was very familiar with from experiencing them so many years of my life. This time, though, one thing was different. This time, I had a place where I could run for help. It was help with people who truly wanted to help in anyway they could. They were not only people outside of me, but I could feel a place of peace within me within the crazy feeling. Jesus was bringing me peace beyond all understanding. It was there beneath the surface, my foundation. It held me together as I told my kids on Sunday what had happened. They had to live out the rest of their lives without their dad.

That feeling of peace in the middle of chaos was so foreign to me. It was great but I didn't understand where it was coming from. That fall, I started going to a Bible study. I felt really stupid even thinking about joining it. I thought, "Those people have the Bible memorized. I don't even know how to open the book. I don't know the first thing about it." In hindsight, it was a really great experience and brought me more and more peace in the chaos of life.

After developing those relationships in church and Bible study, the next January, they offered a trip to Kenya. I finally had the nerve to at least look into it and then say yes to going. It took my life in every way to a whole new, higher level. You can read or listen more about that in my book *From Lawyer to Missionary: A Journey to Kenya and Back Again* and the sequel to that book, *From Lawyer to Missionary: The Journey Continues.*

Healing through the emotional healing workshops brought me to my need for spiritual healing. At the base of all of this, I have found spiritual healing is the most important. It is the peace in the inner-most level of your being. If change is made there, it will last forever and even beyond this life here on earth.

The Kenya mission trip started a whole new journey of spiritual healing for me. However, this full story fills a whole other book. For our purposes here, it was where I found lasting healing outside of my own efforts. I didn't have to control everything and be fearful I was missing things. I discovered this is where full healing starts… the physical and emotional healing can lead us into the final part of healing, which is spiritual healing. I didn't have to read the correct book or watch the right Oprah show. (I still love Oprah though! She was, and is, an inspiration to me.) Jesus gives me what I need when I need it. The Bible has everything I will ever need to lead the best life possible here on earth. I finally learned to fully TRUST.

RECEIVING FORGIVENESS

In this process of gathering my life back, I have found a key part. Without this part, all of the attempts to heal have fallen short and fallen apart. That part is forgiveness.

Forgiveness can be a tough word. Let's start by talking about what forgiveness is not. Forgiveness is NOT saying what happened was right or OK. Forgiveness is NOT giving up pursuing legal action against the person who did this. Forgiveness is NOT continuing an unhealthy relationship. Forgiveness is NOT forgetting what happened. Put those thoughts about forgiveness aside, and open your mind to what forgiveness is.

Let's start by remembering there are things in life that we need forgiveness for. It can be for the things you have done. Maybe you had an abortion, were involved in drugs or alcohol, or you said things that you shouldn't have. The maybes are endless. We all have things we need to be forgiven for. Search for yours.

If you ask for forgiveness from Jesus, you are forgiven. It doesn't matter what you think or feel about it. You are forgiven, if you ask. If you go on pretending you are perfect, justifying your reasons, blaming, and thinking you don't need forgiveness, that's a problem. It is called pride. However, if you ask for forgiveness, you are forgiven. Live in that forgiveness. Don't live in guilt, shame, and condemnation anymore. Step out. Ask, receive, and live in the freedom forgiveness offers you!

As for my story, I have made some life choices I definitely regret, but I know I am forgiven by the One who matters. Some may not understand the choices I made. Some may stand in judgment on me for them. That is their choice. To be honest, I don't even agree with some of the choices I made. However, I know I am forgiven. I know I don't have to, and won't, live in their guilt or my shame. Jesus died to forgive me for my poor choices. I believe in him and have asked him for that forgiveness. He has granted it to me. I'm moving on to become more and more like Him everyday. I am leaving those things behind.

I hope you will join me. If you do not, you will keep circling the same pain, guilt, and shame. You will do it over and over and over again. Confess it and leave it behind you—where it belongs! Receive forgiveness for yourself.

GIVING FORGIVENESS

Forgiveness is letting go of resentment, bitterness, and rage, and committing that person to God for their punishment. It is letting go of my right to hurt another person for hurting me. This is not an easy step, but once you do it, you will be truly free. You will need God's help to do it.

I want to once again clarify what forgiveness is not. Forgiveness does not mean you do not pursue legal action against the person. I encourage you to pursue legal action, both to gain your power back and to help protect others from that person. Forgiveness does not mean the person doesn't have consequences for their actions. It just means YOU are not personally responsible for ensuring that the person pays for what they have done.

Giving forgiveness is where we justify our resistance. "They don't deserve it." However, the bitterness/resentment you keep for them is keeping the person tied to you. The person you most want to be free from is constantly controlling your mind and thoughts. I don't want that for you. I want you to be free and to be able to control your own mind and thoughts.

Once you forgive them, there is nothing left to hold you to them. If you do not forgive, it is a prison that you lock yourself into. You stuff their words, thoughts, and actions into your precious heart. You then hold them there. You lament over them. You scream about them. You hate them. You think about them over and over and how unfair it is.

However, in reality you are keeping yourself stuck in a prison. It is a prison only you have the key to. You lock yourself inside a cell surrounded by these people and their thoughts, words, and actions. Once you let them go – YOU are free. They have to stand before God for their actions and is no longer your problem. YOU free yourself.

If you choose forgiveness, you will not regret one moment of it.

HOW TO FORGIVE

First of all, there is no right or wrong way to forgive. Remember forgiveness is not a one-and-done act. It is not bad or wrong if you continue to have thoughts of the events or person. The key is to continue to remember to forgive over and over again. This is especially true at the beginning. It does get easier with time. However, just because thoughts keep coming up in your mind, does not mean you have not "properly" forgiven. It just means you have to keep forgiving, which is normal. When those thoughts come up, I would encourage you to replace the thoughts with your dreams. Start thinking more about those things and less on these things. You must help to retrain your mind to focus on YOU and not them.

I have a few ideas about specific actions to take to help facilitate forgiveness. The most effective thing for me was to write a letter I was never going to send. I wrote a letter into which I poured all of my anger, sadness, and everything that was stolen from me. It is important to take all of the details and to pour them all out. Don't try to make this perfect–just pour it out. Let the tears flow. Let the bitterness run. Let the hurt out.

We cannot fully accept love from others until we get rid of all this trash.

I then wrote a part of the letter acknowledging they probably had similar things done to them in their childhood to think and act like this. It was remembering that hurt people hurt other people. I did not excuse their behavior toward me in anyway. I just acknowledged they have hurts too. That's all.

This does not mean you don't pursue legal action. This step here is to simply take the negative charge out of YOU about this person. By remembering they were once hurt, it helps us to remember they are a whole person that has some good and some bad in them. It helps us to move on. That is all. It is not an excuse to let them off the hook for their actions. It is simply placing them in the proper order in our mind.

Prayer is the other part of the forgiveness process. It involves remembering God will take care of matters and make all things right. It requires focusing more on who you are (including your hopes, dreams, and future) and less on who they are and what they have done. It is NECESSARY to change your thoughts, which can be helped with prayer. Reading the Bible and being around people who are immersed in the Word also helps.

AT LAST, MY LIFE BACK

I cannot even begin to write how amazing life has become since spiritual healing. I am doing things I never dreamed of doing. I have been traveling the world several times a year and most importantly, living a life free of fear. At this point, I have regained control over my body. No one controls it and I do not turn it over to others. I will stand strong when I need to and I will not enter a situation I don't feel comfortable entering. No one can force me into that. Sometimes, I need to push myself into situations – like writing or speaking about things like this, but no one else can push me into it. No one can take my power away.

Most of the physical symptoms are gone. The mouth issues with cankersores and other things were over shortly after childhood. The strep throat would rear its head in finals during law school. However, other than that, it has not been an issue. The migraines are still a bit of an issue for me, but not as big as they were in childhood. I now only get migraines when I push myself too hard for too long wanting to help more and more people overcome their life struggles.

I have my mind back. As I've shared throughout the book, my memory returned and I have owned those experiences. This has enabled me to take the emotional charge out of them. I now use them to help others, instead of destroying myself.

My thoughts are my own. They are my responsibility. Hope is a way of thinking. I have a choice every second what to think about. I can choose to focus on the good things happening around me or obsess over the bad. I can choose gratitude for what I have and hold loosely what I want. I don't have to allow my emotions to take control of my thoughts. I choose what to think about and keep my mind on. I choose carefully. After awhile, it turns more automatic after you reprogram your thoughts from fear and dread. Some of the things I do to keep this mindset are reading a good book, reading the Bible, talking with a friend, or journaling to keep my thoughts in line. I'm careful about the movies or TV I watch and what I allow into my mind. This prevents me from distracting myself back into fear.

My emotions are my own. No one tells me how to feel or what to feel. No one can force me into any emotion I do not allow. My emotions are decisions, not the result of other people's actions or inactions. If my husband does or says something that makes me angry, I can choose to yell. I can also choose to walk away and address it later when I'm calmer. It might lead to a better result. I can get angry without freaking out about it getting out of control. I can admit that I'm sad at times and take steps to watch a funny TV show or something else to change things around for me. I don't have to rely on anyone else to form or fix my emotions for me.

Perfectionism has been turned upside down. Since my connection with Jesus, I am very happy to admit that I am FAR from perfect. I am the furthest from perfect that one can get. That is just fine. It is in my imperfection where God comes in to help me. If I were perfect, I wouldn't need Him. Anyway, it is beyond any words I could describe: the freeing feeling of being able to admit I am not perfect and openly share and admit my faults, habits, and hang-ups. There's nothing left to hide.

To be real with people, it is necessary to allow them to love me, BECAUSE of the imperfections, not IN SPITE of them. People relate to imperfect. We are all imperfect people. By embracing imperfection, I have found connection, compassion, and courage. My imperfections do not equal inadequacy now–they are a reminder that we are all in this together. I am so happy I am free now to admit that!

My relationships have been healed. I shared earlier that relationships have been a real and constant struggle for me. After finding healing myself, I could accept others that brought value to the table also could love and care about me for me. I met my amazing husband, Chris, in 2006. We have been through our ups and downs, just as in any relationships, especially since we both had school-aged children at the time. Yet, we are now happier in 2017 than we were in 2006 when we first met. Even through struggles, we support and love each other. Sometimes, it is in spite of each other. This is only true because Jesus is in the middle of our relationship.

MORE ADDED TO LIFE

There are so many things I have been set free from and the details of all of them or any of them could fill volumes. Here are a few examples of how spiritual healing through Jesus has helped me turn my life from trauma to triumph:

Sadness to Joy

Anxiety to True Peace

Control to Trust

Judgment, Shame, and Guilt to Forgiveness

Terror/Fear to Love

Anger to Gentleness, Patience,and Kindness

Disgust to Goodness

Shame to Enough

Powerless to Power in Him

Secrecy to Freedom in Truthfulness. I have nothing to hide! This is who I am, this is what I've done, and this is what has been done to me. You are free to accept me or move on. That is not a judgment or statement about me. It says more about the person staying or going. I can stand in this firmly, always, only with His help.

MY LIFE NOW

Through writing this book, I have become aware of one of the reasons I am so passionate about the work I do. It is because of voice. I am the voice here in my little part of the world for those who have no voice. I still struggle at times in using my voice for ME, but I have found a voice.

I used my voice after law school to stand up for children and others through court and negotiating in law situations. I now do mission work for Kenya, Africa and use my voice for power, for purpose.

I travel to Kenya two times a year. I share their stories of trauma and ask for financial help in making their stories to triumph through sponsors and prayers. Living without clean water, children and adults starve to death from lack of hydration and food. They suffer in many ways and they have no voice. Not many in the world even look at their troubles. This includes the more financially stable of their own country. They turn their heads the other way. Their government is very corrupt which leaves the situation stagnant. The world (including myself) is/was unaware of their situation. No one looks, no one listens, and no one cares.

God has now led me to be the voice for thousands of women and girls in Kenya who have no voice or no one to listen to their voice. I have started two non-profit organizations–one specifically doing mission work in Kenya–Operation Give Hope. Operation Give Hope has four schools and feeding centers. It gives kids, who otherwise would have no school, the opportunity to go to school. The children selected for our schools are the 3-year-olds in the surrounding communities who are closest to death from starvation.

Our feeding centers provide the only meal many receive all day and all week. Many students come back to school on Monday faint, because they have not eaten all weekend. Operation Give Hope also has a medical dispensary at one of our schools. It is similar to an urgent care center in the United States. We also have two "Rescue Centers," which are similar to an orphanage. All of these efforts give life and voice to thousands of kids and families.

My passion project is a Women's Crisis Center - Mercy's Light: House Of Hope. We are currently building the center, which is specifically for girls who are pregnant as the result of incest or rape. We are helping them through that trauma as well as providing education, job training, and housing as needed.

I have also started a non-profit called Infinitely More. At Infinitely More, we do many things. The point of all our work is to let people, like you, know that there is life after trauma. There is a good life. You are not alone. Together, we can overcome.

Who would have thought that the shy, withdrawn girl of her primary school years would now be on television and standing in front of a lot of people, sharing other people's stories? The power of healing! This can be true for you as well.

LIFE CYCLES

That is not to say I don't go through periods where things are rough. Writing this book brought up areas in which I still remain stuck in many ways. However, I can now deal with it and I have strategies. I have a support system and a community willing to help me. I am honest about my life, my feelings, and my circumstances. I don't need to hide ANYTHING! I can reach out for help!

Healing happens in circles. You are never complete. You will keep going around and around on the circle of healing all of your life. To know I am at least moving on the circle is tremendously freeing!

The experiences of rape and sexual abuse are now a part of me, but they don't define me. For most of my life, they did define me. Then I defined me, which caused me more anxiety and stress. Now, Jesus defines me by what he says about me in the Bible. Life is free when I choose to live that way.

HELPING OTHERS

My heart now only hurts for those who are still stuck. They are stuck in emotional pain and pretending it is not affecting them. Those people are still stuck with the actual attacks continuing to happen in their lives. My heart aches for those people. I'm actually grateful for my experience, so I can help others. Hopefully, they won't have to stay stuck in the muck as long as I did. I wouldn't be doing what I am doing and loving it if this hadn't happened.

As a coach, I had the opportunity to share with an athlete who shared her struggles. I have been meeting with a homeless woman (under some freeway underpasses) in my hometown. I have no idea what her full story is. However, the look in her eyes and an internal connection makes me believe she has been through some similar situations. I cannot walk by and let others suffer in their pain.

Another opportunity to share happened in the middle of writing this book. We were doing an event for Kenya and the flyer had the words "Proceeds save the lives of girls pregnant by rape or incest and their babies in Mombasa, Kenya." We received word that a principal at an elementary school refused to hand out the flyer, because it had the words, rape and incest, on it. At first glance, it seemed like he was protecting his kids, which is a good thing.

However, those words are actually not "bad words." Those are not words any child should be ashamed of or afraid to hear. By trying to hide the words, it leaves one in four girls in his classroom sitting in silence. The acts are being done to them. They just don't have the words to describe it. By keeping those words hidden, he is actually helping the perpetrator keep all these things secret. That is exactly what the abusers want. Meanwhile, that poor little girl sits in her kindergarten classroom with it happening to her every night, but not having any words available to her to describe it.

These are the things that keep me sharing. These are the things that stir more passion in me.

***

There is hope. There is help. I hope this story has brought you to the place of hope. I hope you will reach out for healing. Don't let my story be the end of the line for you. It is time for you to start your own healing journey. If I can do this, so can you. Let's do this together!

Your story may be exactly like mine, or it may be totally different from mine. Maybe it was a boy at school who raped you, or maybe your trauma isn't sexually related. Whatever the story behind your experience, the healing process will be very similar.

Name it.

Talk about it to a counselor.

Own It.

Tell it to help others.

Acknowledge the damage done.

Let it go.

The good news is if you are willing to enter the healing process and work at it, you will find healing, no matter what the story behind your experience is.

How did I get here? I shared a little bit earlier, but really the biggest thing was Jesus. Knowing the truth about what He did, dying on the cross, being buried and rising again. And why He did it—because he loved ME. He gave me the courage not only to get healing for myself through therapy and classes, but also to reach out and share my story with others to bring them healing as well.

PROLOGUE:

WHERE TO GO FROM HERE?

I hope after this journey of hope and healing, you realize you're not alone.

I hope this book has helped you in the journey.

I hope you want to find a free life.

Don't wait!

Healing does take time and commitment. However, if you are willing to make the investment, you WILL have healing. I would encourage you to seek out a psychologist or other therapist, as well as emotional healing experiences. The Center for Creative Learning has very good programs in the Milwaukee area and nationwide. Don't stop at your emotional and physical healing–make sure you also make the jump to spiritual healing. Find a local church who loves you right where you are.

KEEP WORKING AT IT. IT'S NOT A ONE-TIME THING

You won't forget the traumatic experience and that's OK. But you will not feel the emotional charge that you used to feel from the experience and thoughts.

It is very important to share our stories. At some points in our history, people would not talk about their cancer for fear of judgment and shame. Now we hear those stories and we are comfortable with them. The same can be true of sexual abuse and rape, but only if we are willing to share our stories and let people know they are not alone in this journey.

Writing this book has brought me even further out of shame from the stuck emotions and behaviors.

Having the first few drafts read by someone was scary, but at the same time, it freed me. Every time you share your story, it takes the power from the experience and puts it back in YOU.

As you go through this journey, always remember you are not alone. You are loved, and you are beautiful just the way you are, right now, today. You are as beautiful as you ever were. Please share your stories with me as you go. My contact information is at the back of this book.

Also, stay tuned for further books, coaching, and workbooks that may help you with your healing.

MY BODY STOLEN: MY STORY

I start with a warning. This is graphic and has lots of detail. I want you to know my situation, so you realize I can relate to yours.

THE FIRST TIME

My first fuzzy memory of sexual abuse is as a toddler. This memory comes to me in triggers. A trigger is something that sets off a memory tape or flashback transporting a person back to the event of the original trauma. According to University of Alberta, Sexual Assault Centre:

Triggers are very personal; different things trigger different people. The survivor may begin to avoid situations and stimuli that trigger a flashback. She/he will react to this flashback and trigger with an emotional intensity similar to the one at the time of the trauma. A person's triggers are activated through one or more of the five senses: sight, sound, touch, smell, and taste.

The first abuse happened in a basement, on a laundry room floor. I was on the floor next to where the bleach was stored. The smell of bleach brings me right back to that freezing cold floor. My body tenses up with fear. It is my greatest trigger. At the beginning of my journey, I did not realize the reason for this feeling that overcame my body when I smelled bleach. In fact, I thought everyone reacted that way to bleach.

Years later, acknowledging the intensity of the reaction to the smell of bleach was abnormal, I sat with that for a minute and it sparked specific photograph still-shot memories of the event for me. Pictures popped into my head of laying in the laundry room area.

143

<table>
<tr><td>

PHOTO ONE:

Lying on the thin, rubber mat that was on the ground near the washing machines in the basement with the smell of bleach lofting in the air.

</td><td>

PHOTO TWO:

Trying to scream, but his hand was held up to my face; biting his hand and then being slapped.

</td></tr>
<tr><td>

PHOTO THREE:

Him laying on top of me with all of his weight

</td><td>

PHOTO FOUR:

Wiggling and using my hands to push him and my legs to kick him in an attempt to get away.

</td></tr>
</table>

PHOTO FIVE:

The photo that would flash from this trigger was him sitting on my chest, cutting off my ability to scream with his weight, and him putting his penis in my face and mouth

I could not scream. I don't remember most of the words, since I was too young. When I smell bleach, these are the photos that would rise up and be opened in my mind.

Photo four leads to my second greatest trigger for these early events. The second trigger point is someone holding my wrists together in one hand. In trying to get control of me, he would grab both of my little arms in one hand and hold them up over my head. Then he would shift from laying on top of me to sitting on my chest with his penis in my face and mouth, holding my wrists together in one hand.

From the position of sitting on my chest, it was not possible to penetrate my other areas; therefore, he chose oral sex. It kept me quiet, while at the same time he got what he wanted, using my body to fulfill his sexual desires.

The only words I remember are, "You will be in trouble if you tell anyone. You are being very naughty right now."

Another trigger point for me that is less strong but obvious looking back over my life, is problems with my mouth. It is nothing serious, but canker sores, an extreme gag reflex with phlegm on dental visits, inability to swallow pills, among other things. I would regularly have strep throat, especially on Christmas and my birthday.

These events started as a toddler and continued until I was around 5-years-old. The assaults would happen on holidays and other family events. I do my best every year to psych myself up for the holidays. Some years I do a pretty good job early in the season. However, when it comes to the day of the holiday my mind is a mess. Most of it is not even conscious. I feel depressed, down, and do not want to be around people. There is no reason why. I just am. It happens every year.

WHAT HAPPENED NEXT?

Nothing.

I did nothing and said nothing. I was too little to have a frame of reference. How does a three, four, or five year old explain having sex to someone? There are no words. We don't use words to help little ones define these experiences. This leads to increased under-reporting and leaves kids stuck in situations they don't even know how to talk about. Teach kids the proper names of body parts and not to be ashamed of their bodies as early as they speak and at a level they can understand.

That was me, naughty and silent. I heard my kindergarten teacher talked to my parents about my extremely withdrawn behavior. Nothing ever came of it and during my kindergarten year of school, my abuser passed away.

THE SECOND TIME

Fast-forward many years. I remember this incident with graphic detail. However, for several years, right after it happened, I blocked out all of the details. The memory came flooding back a few years later. I was almost ten years old. He was four years older. We were playing Simon and Risk in his bedroom during a family birthday party. We were all having a good time. It was the same as we had done many times before. Since he was family, I trusted him. If you couldn't trust family, who could you trust?

Then he asked, "Do you want to play doctor?"

I asked, "What is that?"

"You lay back here," he said, pointing to the small space behind the bed just before the wall of his L-shaped bunk bed.

I did not think anything of it. I figured it was just another game, like Operation or something. So, I hopped back there. He hopped on the bed with his head leaning over the edge of the bed, up from where I was laying.

Then he said, "Pull your pants down, just a little bit. Then I rub you like this. Doesn't that feel good?"

I didn't answer him. I just laid there. He continued to talk as he touched me. He told me, "You can't tell anyone about this, because if you do, they will be mad at you. They don't want you to feel this good, and you will get into a lot of trouble."

This went on for a year or so. We only got together at holidays and for birthdays a few times a year. Then about a year later, we were at another cousin's house. It was birthday time. I remember I got a cat for my birthday, and it was the best present ever. I had wanted a cat for years.

I had just turned 12 and was in the 5th grade. We hadn't even had the period/sex talk that you get in school yet. We were in the basement playing hide-and-go-seek in the dark and were all having a fun time. I loved that they accepted me. Next, he said, "Let's go play doctor in the closet." I didn't want to, but I wanted to be accepted. Therefore, I did what he said. It was a big, empty walk-in closet. They were doing a remodel of the basement, and it had an overhead light in it with an on/off switch at the door. I pulled my pants and underwear down just above my knees. I remember lying down with my feet facing the west toward the door of the closet and my head facing the east, to the back of the closet.

Right away, it felt different. He told someone, "Go keep watch at the door and turn off the light." Then he laid down next to me on my right side, which was not normal. He never would lay down by me. That's not how this worked.

By then my eyes had adjusted to the dark and I could see and hear him unzip his own pants and pull them down, exposing his soft, limp penis. I didn't know what was going on. He quickly started rubbing up against the outside of my upper thighs and his penis started taking on more of a shape. I was so scared I couldn't even speak.

He got on top of me and rubbed his penis between my thighs. He then quickly moved it over to my genital area. It was getting firm now. He kept moving back and forth with his penis sliding between my thighs and my genitals. Every time it came up to my genitals, I kept moving back. It hurt so much when he pushed. I didn't understand what he could possibly be doing. He was getting mad because it wasn't working. I had no idea what was going on.

He yelled to the door person, "Turn on the light! I can't do this in the dark. I cannot see anything and it is way too small!" At that point, he was on top of me and trying to get his erect penis inside me. It was hot, gross, and scary. It was a little wet at times and I didn't understand where that wetness was coming from. I thought he had peed.

It hurt so badly. When I was finally able to talk, I said, "This hurts really bad." He took a break from his anger and frustration long enough to say, "It will be OK once we get started. It will feel a lot better just like when I was touching you. That felt good, didn't it?" I was silent for a while and he continued to struggle.

Then I started crying, "It hurts, please stop, it hurts." He was frustrated, but he tried to enlist my help, "If you want it to stop hurting and feel like it did before, you need to bend your knees and spread your legs apart a little bit." He pulled my underwear and pants down more and repositioned me at what he thought was a better angle. That didn't work either and I was still crying, "Stop, it hurts, stop."

"Stop crying! You're too small," he yelled. "Why won't this work? … Stop moving!" He was pulling and pushing on me, trying to get himself inside of me.

I didn't want him to hit me. I wanted this over with. I wanted it to stop, so I tried to help. "Stop crying," he said. So I did, out loud at least. "Move down more," he said. So I did. "Lie still." So I did. With everything I had, I pushed myself into the floor in an effort to not move when he tried to get inside of me. It hurt so much. I started crying again.

"Bend your knees up more. Spread your legs more. I need more room for this. You're so small." He kept at it and kept at it. I obeyed his every command, praying that at least he wouldn't hit me.

Finally, the look-out person opened the door and yelled, "Stop, stop, someone is coming." He turned the light off and shut the door again.

Back in the room, he was angry. He apparently hadn't done what he came here to accomplish. He was frustrated. "I should make you suck me, but we don't have time now," he said in disgust. "Get dressed and get out of here. You're useless anyways. You're way too small. Hurry up before someone finds you and you get yourself into trouble. Remember, you will be the one in a lot of trouble, if someone finds out," he said in a voice full of confidence.

I rushed to pull my pants up and ran upstairs to the bathroom. I went to the bathroom, dizzy and confused. It was as if the room was spinning. When I wiped… I wiped blood and started crying. I didn't know what to do, but I did know I couldn't tell anyone, so I couldn't ask for help.

Even if I wanted to tell, I wouldn't know what to say. I didn't even know what had just happened. All I knew was it hurt and it felt horrible. It never crossed my mind to tell anyone. Tell someone? Tell them what? I didn't even know what had happened.

Eventually I pulled myself together enough to sit upstairs with the adults. I had to do something. I felt totally numb.

From that Sunday afternoon on, my life would never be the same. I didn't know why or even what had changed, but I knew something inside me had changed. When this happened, I turned from the cute, fun-loving, pig-tailed blonde to a bags-under-my-eyes, solemn-all-the-time shadow of a person. You could see it in my school pictures between the 4th and 5th grades. There was a physical difference in who I was. It was as if all of me had been stripped out–mind, soul, and spirit. All that was left was an empty shell of a body walking around.

THE THIRD TIME

When I was 14-years-old, my parents were building a house. However, the new house was not ready by the time the old house sold. We were staying at friend's and relative's houses until it was done. Depending on what we were doing the next day, we would stay at different houses. One night, we were to sleep at his house. To be honest, I don't remember being afraid or even specifically nervous. It had been almost three full years since it had happened, and in my head it was so far below the surface of my mind's thoughts, it was like it had never happened. I had completely blocked it out.

The day was coming to a close and I asked where I should sleep. They said to sleep in his room. My aunt didn't think he would be home that night. So I changed into my nightgown, went to bed and fell asleep.

In the middle of the night, I woke up and quickly realized he was there. I was lying on my left side, facing the window of his room. He was right against me, facing me. My night gown was right above my underwear line.

He was holding his naked penis and rubbing his semi-hard form up and down my thighs and between my legs. He was taller than me, so his head was above mine on the bed. I hoped he could not see my face to know my eyes had opened. I was afraid to let him know I was awake. What would he do? Would he get mad? Would he hit me? Would he force himself on me? So I just lay there, afraid.

He continued. At times, he would rub the tips of my breasts under my nightgown. He continued to rub his harder penis, mostly between my legs now. The only thing between his penis and my genitals was my underwear. I was grateful for this barrier. I was too afraid to act, not knowing what he would do, and at the same time feeling guilty and conflicted.

Finally, after I don't know how long, I decided my best bet would be to simply turn over onto my other side so I was facing away from him and pretend to still be asleep and just lie there. I reasoned he could not do anything to me, if my back was towards him. "That should take care of it," I thought. I was so, so scared. However, I made the move, rolling over onto my right side facing away from him and to the wall. "It worked," I thought. No big scene and now he couldn't do anything to me because the parts he wanted were away from him.

I was silently enjoying my moment of victory in my head when all of a sudden he was behind me stretching his full body down the length of mine and beyond. When he was done arranging himself, his now hard penis was resting between my thighs. At first he just laid there, as though he was waiting for me to either get comfortable with it, or to fall asleep again.

Then ever so slowly, as though he were testing the waters to see if I was asleep, he started moving his penis back and forth against my thighs. Then he started to push it between my thighs harder and harder.

In my own head, I was again trying to run through my "safe" options. Continue to fake sleep? What would he do to me if I tried to get up? Would he pin me down? What would he do? What could I do? I felt hopeless and afraid. Fear gripped me so bad, I couldn't even move. By this point, his penis was getting so hard against my thighs it felt like he was going to take it to another level or something. I thought to myself this is my chance; he seems distracted by something. I quickly got up out of the bed and hurried out of the room. I moved fast down the hall to the room where my parents were sleeping. I laid there on the floor, next to their bed for the rest of the night quietly crying, afraid to fall asleep and worried he would come and find me.

RESOURCES TO HELP YOU WITH HEALING:

1. *The Hem of His Garment* – Healing Hearts – online study or through a church. Gets you through any and all possible lifetime trauma.

2. *Breaking Free* & *Believing God* workbook and videos available for purchase online or as a set, Beth Moore.

3. *Beginning to Heal: A First Book for Survivors of Child Sexual Abuse*, Ellen Bass and Laura Davis.

4. *You Can Heal Your Life*, Louise Hay.

5. *Growing Beyond Survival: A Self-Help Toolkit for Managing Traumatic Stress*, Elizabeth G. Vermilya.

6. *Journey to Wholeness: Healing from the Trauma of Rape*, Vicki Aranow and Monique Lang.

7. *The Unburdened Heart: Five Keys to Forgiveness and Freedom*, Mariah Burton Nelson.

8. **InfinitelyMoreLife.org**
   Also, follow Infinitely More Life on Facebook
   for Carrie Reichartz's hope and encouragement.

ORGANIZATIONS:

1. Rape, Abuse, & Incest National Network Hotline - R.A.I.N.N.
   www.rainn.org   1-800-656-4673

2. National Teen Dating Abuse Helpline
   www.loveisrespect.org   1-866-331-9474

3. National Suicide Prevention Lifeline
   www.suicidepreventionlifeline.org   1-800-273-8255

4. Joyful Heart Foundation
   www.JoyfulHeartFoundation.org

   Mariska Hargitay (Olivia on Law & Order: SVU) is the president and founder. Mission: to heal, educate and empower survivors of sexual assault… and to shed light into the darkness that surrounds these issues. Have a magazine available– "Reunion."

5. Center for Creative Learning
   www.Lightly.com

   Taking It Lightly is an emotional intelligence weekend workshop designed to assist you in releasing deeply-held life decisions that are no longer working for you.

ABOUT CARRIE REICHARTZ, AUTHOR

Carrie Reichartz is a lawyer, small business owner, and now nonprofit executive in New Berlin, Wisconsin USA, where she was born and raised. She is wife to Chris, mom to Colton and Brooklyn, and step-mom to Lexie and Zach. She graduated from UW-Whitewater with a BS in psychology/criminal justice and received her law degree from Marquette University Law School in Milwaukee, Wisconsin.

Because of her early childhood trauma experiences, Carrie has always had a passion for working with and for children, hoping to protect them so what happened to her didn't happen to them. She has worked as a guardian ad litem representing children's rights in court as a practicing lawyer for seven years. She has written for several legal publications and, shortly after being voted by her peers as a *Rising Stars* lawyer, she went to Kenya for the first time on a mission trip with Fox River Christian Church in 2008.

After her return, Carrie closed her law office to open a home day care so she could be closer to her children when their dad passed away unexpectedly. This also left more time to work on international issues. Currently, she travels to Kenya two to three times per year and is developing Mercy's Light: House of Hope, a Woman's Crisis Center near Mombasa - the first of its kind. Right now, most girls are kicked out of their homes and schools when it is found they are pregnant. They are left to the streets and prostitution or sex trafficking to feed themselves.

While in Kenya, Carrie spends time in orphanages, rescue centers, boys' homes, schools, and more. She interacts with the kids and with the staff, bringing projects to do together and sharing in their talents of music and more. She takes people with her on trips to Kenya as well.

After the Ebola scare in the media in 2014, Carrie closed her home day care business so she could raise awareness and funds full time for the girls of Kenya.

She speaks in public and private schools, home school groups, women's events, civic organizations, libraries, and more. Topics that Carrie speaks on include: Trauma to Triumph, overcoming rape and sexual abuse, "Poverty Around the World", "A Day in the Life of a Woman in Kenya", "How Flip Flops are Bringing People to Christ in Kenya", overcoming trauma and she also builds specialized topics around event themes.

LET'S STAY CONNECTED!

To help us heal the world, go to www.InfinitelyMoreLife.org.
Subscribe to our newsletter to receive FREE gifts!

Carrie Reichartz – personal page
InfinitelyMoreLife

Carrie Reichartz - author page

CONTINUE YOUR HEALING AND FIND YOUR PURPOSE!

FREE BONUS EBOOK waiting for you at InfinitelyMoreLife.org
24 Day Journey to Healing & Life Purpose written by Carrie.
Specific exercises to help you start or continue your healing.
Get your hands on this valuable tool today.

***

Bring the Trauma to Triumph message to your groups to encourage and inspire. Invite Carrie and others to come speak to your group.

Speaking for preschool through adults

Carrie is available to speak to you and your group or school

Topics vary "I Just Want My Life Back: Triumph over Trauma", "A Day in the Life of a Woman in Kenya", "How Flip Flops are Bringing People to Christ in Kenya". Carrie can build a topic around your theme.

School presentations include "A Day in the Life of Edgar, a Kenyan Child" from shopping to shoes, to school, to shelter. We will compare our lives and what life is like for a child in Kenya. I can show you how to make a difference!

Go to InfinitelyMoreLife.org to book your event today!

COMING SOON: group and individual coaching, courses, and webinars, groups and so much more to help you on your journey of healing. Watch the website and social media for updates!

LIVE THE KENYAN ADVENTURE
WITH CARRIE

Read Carrie's other books! Sales from all the books support the trauma healing work we are doing in Kenya.

Available at Amazon or at OperationGiveHope.Etsy.com.

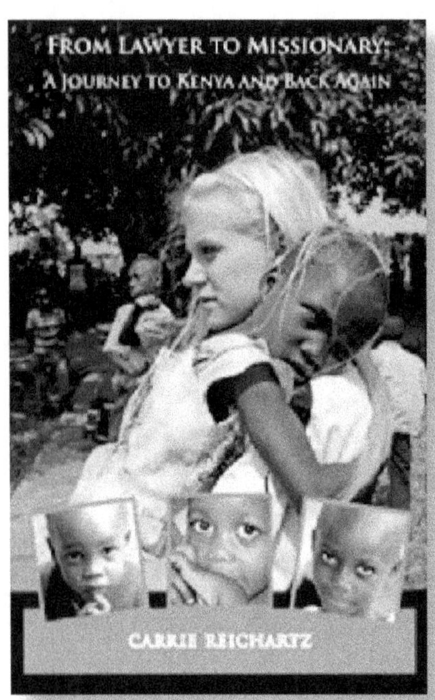

From Lawyer to Missionary:
A Journey To Kenya
And Back
(Audio version of the book is available as well)

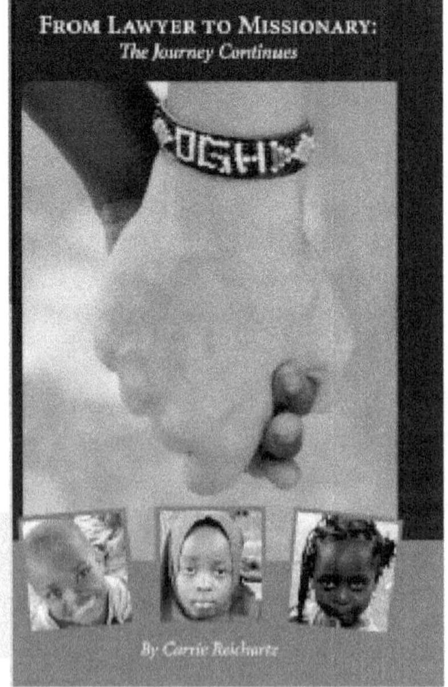

From Lawyer to Missionary:
A Journey Continues

COMING SOON: A CHILDREN'S BOOK!

Do the Leaves Change Color in Kenya, Too?
-Carrie Reichartz

Come on a mission trip with us to Kenya, if you qualify!
Send in your application today!

HELP US SUPPORT LOCAL KENYAN WOMEN SELLING THEIR *CURIOS.*

VISIT TODAY:
InfinitelyMoreLife.etsy.com

Purchase Kenyan treasures – paper bead necklaces, jewelry, prints made out of pieces of banana leaves, bags and purses, hand-carved nativity sets, and so much more. Items change constantly!

All proceeds from these sales go back to Kenya to save the lives of pregnant girls and their babies through Mercy's Light: House Of Hope!